Trail Cool
Made Gourmet

MW01195577

By Sarah Kirkconnell and Matthew "Kirk" Kirkconnell
www.trailcooking.com

**Bay Street
Publishing**

A Division of Bay Street Communications, LLC

Trail Cooking: Trail Food Made Gourmet

Published by Bay Street Publishing, a part of Bay Street Communications, LLC.

Trademarks:

Warranty and Disclaimer:

Other Information:

Additional writing, editing, book layout and design by Matthew Kirkconnell

Cover Design by Sarah Kirkconnell

Cover Photography by Matthew Kirkconnell

ISBN 10: 0-9779249-3-9

First Edition: January 2014

To Kirk, thank you for being my test subject, and not snickering too loudly when I get excited over new recipe ideas.

To Cat and Dani, for encouraging me often and helping me out. You helped me work through many things that had me feeling uninspired.

To my kids, for eating my creations, and for being my hiking partners.

To my readers, thank you for reading, sharing and trying my recipes. And for your feedback and comments, on our blog and Facebook pages. The community we hikers and bloggers have built is amazing. I wouldn't have had this amazing part of my life without all of you!

Introduction

This book took a long time. So long, that I know some of our readers felt it was comparable with Guns n' Roses ever putting out a new album. I will be honest, life got in the way. I was so busy creating new ideas, scratching them down and then out hiking, that I never pulled my manuscripts together. Then I took a 4-year break with backpacking, and had my two youngest children. It's hard to feel excited over writing a book about something you can't get out to do.

2013 brought back my old life, just a bit. Being able to get back out backpacking once again brought my inspiration levels back up. I felt inspired and got back to creating what I had long promised to our readers.

What is Trail Cooking? When we started Freezer Bag Cooking in 2004, I realized by 2006 I wanted more. I didn't want to just be tied down to creating FBC meals for the trail. As Freezer Bag Cooking morphed into www.TrailCooking.com in 2007, I had so many ideas. A full cookbook for the outdoors, with a gourmet touch, yet made easy so most anyone can cook and eat great while outside, without having to carry a massive (heavy) kitchen setup. With over 275+ recipes to choose from, you will have inspiration for many trips to come.

Most of all enjoy your time outside and eat well!

~Sarah Kirkconnell, December 2013

When we started developing recipes for outdoor cooking nearly everything for the first couple years were for the method called Freezer Bag Cooking or also known as FBC. When asked, "What is FBC?" the answer is it is making your own meals, just the way you want. Consider them to be similar to commercial freeze-dried meals but without the cost and you can customize them exactly to how you want!

How to do FBC:

Most people who do the FBC method will package their meals at home before the trip. You will want to note on each bag what the meal is and how much water is required. Some will tuck a tiny note inside; others use a permanent marker on the outside.

When getting ready to "cook" your meal, bring your water to a near boil. Pour the water into your cup to measure, and then add it to your freezer bag. This way you avoid the chance of burns, adding too much water, or touching your freezer bag with a burning hot piece of metal - and having the small potential of melting the bag. You DO NOT need boiling water to rehydrate meals! Boiling is at 212°, 180° water will work just fine. If you need to boil your water to remove any chance of water-born pathogens, let it cool for a couple of minutes and then proceed.

Stir with a long handled metal, wooden or heat safe plastic spoon. After you have mixed it well, zip up the bag tightly and wrap in a fleece hat, jacket or cozy made for the purpose. Then let sit for 5 to 15 minutes (the recipe and altitude will determine how long), make yourself a drink and wait for your meal. Once ready, stir well and eat. We usually put our freezer bag into our cozies before we add the water (since we use a dedicated cozy), this works well as we don't have to hold the bag upright while the water is added.

What is a cozy?

A cozy is an insulated item used to keep your food hot while it rehydrates. We make ultra light washable cozies, which can be found at http://www.trailcooking.com/store/fbc-cozies/. A dedicated cozy is an essential in bear country so that food odors do not get on your clothing (some use their hat to insulate meals as an example).

A Note On Squeezing/Kneading Bags:
If you squeeze or knead your bags to mix up the food, be very careful-be sure you have pushed out all the air before you do this. The steam from the hot liquid can cause a build up and your kneading could cause the bag to pop open. For items like mashed potatoes and stuffing kneading if done carefully works well.

The "How Do I Eat Out Of The Bag?" question:
This can take a little practice, but after your food is ready, roll the top 1/3 of the bag down (imagine you are cuffing socks). This will make your bag into its own bowl. If eating soup or chowders, be careful. You can also with a sharp camp knife cut off the top half to make a "bowl".

The "How Do I Feed 2 People?" Question:
Many of the recipes are listed as feeding two people, which might make one wonder, how do you feed 2 out of 1 bag? My answer to this has to been to bring two bags with me - an extra bag (usually recycled from having held dry food before). After the meal is ready, I do the final stirring, and then divide the meal between the two bags.

Insulated mug method:

Similar to using the FBC method, but using an insulated mug, instead of freezer bags. The mug acts as a cozy for you. Follow the FBC method if a recipe does not mention using a mug. The method works best for solo meals for one in the range of 1/2 cup to 1 1/2 cups water added.

It will depend of course on what size mug you carry while backpacking - do you take a 12-ounce mug? Or a 18 ounce one? A 12-ounce mug works best with no more than 1-cup water added to dry ingredients. A 18 ounce mug should be 1 1/2 cups or less water added. You will need room for your food to expand!

If super hungry, there is always the Super Grande coffee mugs found at truck stops across the country. You could fix a meal for a logger in one of those puppies!

You can take any sturdy (yet light) mug that you prefer but you will want a good tight fitting lid. Be it plastic or metal, either is up to you. If you use metal be warned the interior will be cold in winter. Preheating with hot water will be needed to not chill your food.

No Cook Method:

Having meals that need no heat has been very popular in the past couple years. The recipes can make great lunches, an easy meal in bad weather and also they have been extremely popular with long distance hikers looking to save weight on fuel.

Pack your meals at home in a snack, sandwich or pint/quart freezer bag (whatever you prefer). Note the amount of water on the bag in permanent marker and what the meal is or tuck a small note inside.

Depending on the recipe rehydration will be nearly instant to up to 30 minutes. Add in cool water, seal the bag and knead or shake gently. Set aside till ready.

The most traditional method of trail cooking is by using a lightweight pot to cook your meal in. By incorporating the methods of FBC into it you can avoid lengthy cook times (and pot scrubbings) as well you can save fuel. This method is attractive to long distance hikers and to those avoiding the use of plastics.

One Pot Method:

To save time, at home bag each meal up. You can use snack and sandwich bags for this. Be sure to mark with a permanent marker or tuck a small note inside that notes what the meal is and how much water is called for.

Add the water called for, any oil and meat to your pot. In some cases the recipe will call for the dried vegetables or the dried ingredients to be added as well. Follow the recipe directions to be sure. Bring the water to a boil, turn off your stove and add in the dry items. Stir well and cover tightly. At altitude or in cooler temperatures you will want to consider using a pot cozy to insulate your pot (it retains quite a bit of heat in). You can make your own or buy them ready to go from Anti Gravity Gear.

The cleaning of your pot is easier this way than if you do regular cooking, where you simmer for a lengthy time, such as 10 to 20 minutes. When done, wipe out with a paper towel and then rinse with a mild mixture of outdoor safe soap/water. If you use a non-stick pot you often won't need a scrubby pad.

Gear & Tools:

Eating well doesn't mean you need to carry a big kitchen with you on the trail. You needn't carry heavy pans, multiple pans, a lot of fuel, and have to do cleanup after your meals. You can eat great, have a nice variety of foods, and be done eating before dark. There are a few items and techniques that will go a long way to achieving edible nirvana…. or as close as we can get to it.

Basic tools needed:

A backpacking teakettle, or lightweight pot with lid.

For solo you will want capacity of 1 1/2 to 4 cups water. For two you will want at least 4 cups (1 Liter) to 8 cups (a 2 Liter pot). With bigger families or groups you can go as large as a 3 Liter pot but it becomes easier to carry two smaller pots and two stoves - it is often faster that way. Any metal (Titanium, Hard Anodized Aluminum, etc) is fine you will develop a preference over time. If boiling water only your pot need not be non-stick or hard anodized. While not needed for one pot cooking, the coatings make cleanup much easier.

A canister or alcohol stove.

Good brands of canister stoves are MSR, Primus, Coleman, Snowpeak, and Jet Boil and many others. Canister stoves are simple and safe to use, making them a great choice for those who don't like to tinker. Do use name brand fuel, off brands can foul up your stove quickly. If your stove has an electric starter (a Piezo) do pack a backup way to light it. They can and do break! Canister stoves are a good choice for families and when fire bans are on. You rarely get flare-ups and are quick to shut off. Expect issues with performance at high altitudes and in the cold.

Alcohol stoves are very popular due to ease of use - with no parts to break and whisper quiet. They do have a learning curve and should not be used during fire bans or in tinder dry areas (they are an open flame). Do use with caution around children and animals.

White gas/multi fuel stoves. They have their fans for winter use/high altitude adventures. Do know how to field repair them before using one. Expect them to be the messiest of choices. Learn how to light it to avoid flare-ups.

Solid fuel stoves. Usually known under the name Esbit, these minimalist stoves are good for solo hikers who only need to boil a cup or so of water. They work well but can leave a sooty coating on your pot (it washes off with dish soap easily) and have a chemical smell when burning. Practice at home till you get the hang of it.

A windscreen for your stove made of a turkey pan, stove liner pan or heavy-duty foil folded 3 times. This will increase fuel efficiency. Most companies that make alcohol stoves include them with the stove.

FBC Cozy: If you plan on doing meals FBC style you will need something to insulate your meal with. A dedicated cozy is important. You can then tuck it into your food bag at night. Look for lightweight and washable. http://www.trailcooking.com/store/fbc-cozies/

A long handled spoon to eat with. You can find heat safe plastic, wood (and now Bamboo!) and metal. Sporks can be used very carefully if eating pasta dishes. Be careful though with poking the bags.

A mug/cup with measuring markers on it. Dual purpose for your hot beverages, but also for an exact measure for meals. Many mugs made for backpackers have measurement lines.

Paper Towels: Yes, an odd one there but you will find them quite useful. Tear off a paper towel per day and fold into quarters. Pack them in a quart freezer bag. They work great for assembling food on, wiping messes up and as well wiping out a cooking pot to remove leftover food before cleaning.

Lighter and matches. We carry both. In separate areas of our packs.

Bags: We recommend bringing 1 or 2 extra quart freezer bags in your food bag and double bagging dried pasta as it can have sharp ends. You can use brand name freezer bags (avoid dollar store ones), Food Vac bags or 'Boil-In-Bag' bags for FBC meals. For meals prepared in a mug or in a pot feel free to use snack or sandwich size plastic bags. For those avoiding plastics you can buy wax paper "bags" for sandwiches but are not good for powder items. You can as well make bags out of muslin fabric if one was inclined.

A black permanent marker, to write on your bags. Mark what your meal is, and how much water to add. You can also write it on a scrap of paper and stick it inside.

Are there other items?

Of course.... you can end up like Sarah, with many storage bins overflowing with dishes, pepper mills, spatulas, fry pans, baking ovens......

Just start small and build up is the best advice!

Beyond the basics - Buying your pot.

Unless you decide to go 'no cook', eventually you have to break down and get a kitchen set up. It can be very overwhelming, especially if you wander into a large REI and have no clue where to start. Outside of your stove your biggest item to decide on will be your cooking pot(s). But, if you don't have a kitchen setup get the pot before the stove - you want to love your pot most of all and you don't want to be mismatched. Not all stoves and pot sets work well together.

Things to consider when buying a pot:

What kind of metal do you want? This is going to be a big part of your decision. What is your backpacking style like? Do you take everything? Are you trying to go UL? Is your wallet on a diet? Your major choices will be:

Titanium(TI): The darling of light weight packers it does have its pros - it is very thin metal so pots are light. It heats up fast, helping water boil even faster. If unlined you can use metal utensils and scrub pads. Thin walls get blistering hot but don't retain heat well after removing from heat source. Don't let the pot cook dry, the metal will heat super hot and can warp as well as turn new shades, is notorious for frying on food if you take your eyes off the pot or use too hot a stove, you can get non stick versions but again, you have to have a stove that can simmer, high temps can destroy the lining. Isn't much lighter than HAA, is often twice as much in cost but does come in mugs and smaller pots, so for minimalist setups it may be your only option. And Ti has the "cool factor".

Best uses: boiling water or cooking liquids such as stews and soups. Works well with alcohol stoves and high performance canister stoves.

Hard Anodized Aluminum (HAA): The pros of it are light, transfers heat well (retains it, fans it out so your food cooks more evenly), durable, strong and very affordable. Naturally non stick, though some companies add a super slick lining for ease in cleanup. The hard anodizing allows you to cook acidic foods (cleanup should be done promptly as letting acidic foods sit will eventually lead to the finish wearing off) and does not impart any metal taste. Cons are that not all companies make their products thin walled, some pots made of it can be very heavy. You will need to research if your pot is OK for use with metal utensils. Some HAA pots will get scratched, some are fine with it. Find out also if scrub pads are OK to use.

Best use: Overall HAA is your best buy for the majority of uses. Shop carefully to get what you need and to keep it affordable and light.

Stainless Steel: Is not used as much these days, but can still be found. Pros: High quality, nearly indestructible, very inexpensive. Good for base camping, car camping and for melting snow for water in winter. Can use metal utensils and scrub pads. Cons: the weight of the metal makes it not normally a good choice for backpackers.

Best use: Snow melting in winter (very durable, handles can take being exposed to heat), using with campfires, use by those who are hard on gear.

Aluminum: Rarely seen these days and that is NO loss! Plain aluminum was often used in the old days to make "mess kits" sold to Scouts and similar. It was light, but dented easily and often imparted an aftertaste to food and liquids. Can use metal utensils and scrub pads, but you get a "metal" smell on your hands after cleaning. You also have to avoid using acidic foods in it. Avoid it, just not worth it and none of the major companies make anything with it these days, you will mostly find it in "surplus stores" imported from China.

Best use - Honestly? None. Avoid. You really don't want it!

What kind of pot do you want?

So you figured out what material you want, now you need to decide what pot to get. And do you have choices! Every year multiple new pots come out, plenty to dazzle and confuse the heck out of anyone.

There are three basic styles though:

Tall and Narrow - Often used in smaller pot sizes, from 12 ounce mugs to up to 1.8 Liter or so, it works well for boiling water and meals that have liquid. You will often need a longer handled utensil to stir. Can make clean up a pain if you made a messy meal. Works well on alcohol stoves, and narrow canister stoves. Best for 1 to 2 people.

Wide and Shallow - Often seen in larger pots from 1.5 Liter to 2 to 3 or even up to 4 Liters. They work well on remote fed canister stoves, liquid fuel and stable canister stoves and as well on large propane camp stoves for car camping. You can find great options for 1 to as many people as you need. Typically a 2 Liter wide pot can cook for 2 to 3 people. Wide pots are perfect for gourmet cooking, where you need room to move food around. It can make boiling water harder and longer if your stove is made for a narrower pot. Super cheap often equals cheap flimsy plastic handles that can break and melt if exposed to flame.

The kettle - It is low, wide and short but is typically under a Liter. It works well on all stoves and is very stable. Some are for just boiling water; others allow you to cook in them with a wide top opening.

No matter what you decide on make sure that the pot is sturdy and well built. Some off brands cut corners on the handles. You will see floppy metal handles that don't stay put or worse, plastic handles that can melt if used on the wrong stove! Buyer beware, a $25 bargain may well mean you end up buying twice. Or the top of the pot is rolled weird so food gets trapped under (example? Certain versions of the "grease pot" which is a cheap $10 or less "pot" used by some UL hikers)

As well, don't assume that a set will be better than buying pots by the piece. In all honesty, some sets are great (especially if you have no kitchen when you get going) but better to say have a pot for solo trips, one for if you have a partner and one for luxury car camping. It is common to see new backpackers carry everything in a set - if it has 3 pots, they carry all 3, with all 3 lids. Sets have become huge in the past 3 years or so; every one is making them it seems. It makes sense though; it is a great way to offer convenience and value to the customers. But do ask yourself if you will use the waterproof bucket that holds the set, the mugs, plates, etc. before you buy. If No, then just buy the pot and save $20 to 50.

Also ask yourself what you will really cook. If you know you are a committed FBC or freeze dried meal maker, then go as simple and light as you can. A hiker kettle will be your friend! If you swap between FBC and simple one pot meals consider a narrow 1.8 Liter or so pot so you can do both. If you like to cook big gourmet meals, then invest into a large 2 Liter or bigger wide pot for ease of cooking and cleanup. And consider getting non-stick on it for quick and simple cleanup.

Check that the lid sits well, is easy to take off and that most of all, the handle on the pot is VERY secure. Most companies have gotten with the times and gone to securely clicking in/locking handles. You should NOT have to take the handle off the pot to take off the lid except for in the base models or in small mess kits these days. This makes cooking safer as you can hold on to the pot while you stir. Many pots now have drain holes as part of the lid, allowing you to safely drain water when making pasta, it also allows steam to whistle out while you cook giving less boil overs.

Do make sure to test the new pot(s) at home first to make sure you are comfortable with it. Test it outside, on non-level lawn/dirt, in the wind. Make sure you practice lifting the pot fully loaded with water and draining it. This will let you know that you are comfortable with it.

Once you know what you want then you have to match the stove to it. And do make sure they will be compatible. If your pot has coated or plastic handles, a hot alcohol stove can easily lick up the sides and melt them. If you are using an MSR Pocket Rocket stove or similar canister stove, larger and wide pots will not be as stable on the narrow arms. These are things to check out. Bring your pot with you when you shop if you can and test it filled with water for stability.

Protecting Your Food:

Something that happens quite often for people new to the outdoors is the question of "what do I do with my food at night?" This is literally one of the most important decisions you will make when in the outdoors. Do it wrong and you can face being hungry and miserable.

Please remember, YOU are the visitor to the wilds. It is your duty to keep human food and garbage from the animals. A couple years ago, at Mt. Rainier NP, I experienced a bear that had been fed by humans at a trailhead campground, simply because they thought it was cute to do. That bear kept coming back (as they will do) into the front country. Needless to say, I watched the black bear panic and destroy a basically new hood on an innocent hiker's car (it was jumping up and down with claws out). That bear was lucky, it was given 3 chances in being relocating and finally did not come back. Many others though are put down every year. It does NOT have to happen if we are more careful of our presence when visiting the wilds.

We need to protect our food from a wide range of animals: bears, raccoons, coyotes, squirrels, chipmunks, marmots, birds, mice, rats, skunks, etc. Ironically the smallest animals can be some of the worst offenders. Mice drive people in shelters crazy, birds will swoop in. Raccoons can unzip tents and packs to get in.

You have options, but on using them which method depends on where you hike and the regulations. Be sure to read up online and call the rangers office for the latest information. Don't trust guidebooks as they can be out of date by the time it is printed.

Bear canisters:

All you do is pack your food in them and put in or on your pack. In camp you put your food, garbage and smelly toiletries in the canister and leave it near camp. Tree stumps work great if hollow inside, pop it in. Just make sure the canister is not near water or cliffs, so an animal cannot roll it away. Also do not tie the canister to anything. It helps to put bright duct tape or paint on them in case it does get tossed around. A suggestion is to put your name and phone number on the canister in permanent marker or have a business card taped inside. For example, our canister, a Bear Vault, has this info on the outside and offers that we will pay a reward if found (so we can get it shipped back). This is good if you ever have a bear roll your canister away!

On garbage, and storing it. Yes, it is unappetizing. But you have to do it! Gallon freezer bags work well for storing garbage. Pack the garbage bag at night in your canister, with your food also in gallon freezer bags, this way nothing touches.

Canisters are a must for areas with highly habituated bears (ones that have been fed human food and do nightly patrols of backcountry camp sites) and Grizzly bears. Both are undesirable to have in camp. Canisters used according to directions leads to the bears getting no rewards and leaving. They are simple to use and while heavy, are quite worth it. The bonus is you get a backcountry stool as well to sit on.

The Ursack:

We have been using Ursack Bear Bags for over 8 years. Some people do question it since it is a soft sack, your food can be squished if a bear sits or stands on it. But if you carry dry food (like most of the recipes here), that isn't a problem. With an Ursack all you do is tie it off to a tree base with a figure 8 knot or hang from a tree. It depends on where you are and the rules. It holds more than the canisters, and best of all, rolls down and compresses as you eat your food. They are very lightweight and offer a hybrid aluminum insert to put into the sack to form a lightweight "canister". If you choose to use an Ursack realize that you should separate your Ursack from camp at night, more so if you are camping in heavily used areas. In our hiking group, there are at least 20 of us with Ursacks. We go into copses of trees on the edge of alpine meadows; avalanche areas full of downed trees, in the forest go up a couple hundred feet uphill from camp. Most animals that come into camp are coming back because they got fed before. No food in the "normal" areas and they leave. If you do choose to use one, you must learn how to use it right. No complaining allowed if you use it wrong! That means reading the directions and trying it out so you learn how to do a figure 8 knot. DO NOT use in areas with highly habituated bears or with Grizzly bears. Canisters have their places and this is one area.

Rat Sack:

A bag made of fine stainless steel mesh it does a good job of protecting food but needs to be hidden from birds such as Ravens who are crafty. Will work for most animals but not for habituated black bears or Grizzly bears.

Bear bagging:

And you might think "there is no info on it here". Well, that is because Sarah has never been good at bear bagging, she is short and was a flop at baseball. If done right, it does work, but you need trees of the right size and the know how. Personally we recommend that you use an Ursack, Rat Sack or a canister. If you do choose to bear bag, please use a sack that is only used for your food. Practice in a park or your back yard. Learn how to do it in the pouring rain, when you are so cold that you can barely move your fingers...imagine how you can do it, standing in a moat of snow 4 ft. high. Do it at night and make sure that you have friends laughing at you as it takes an hour. Study up on the PCT Method. Do NOT do bear bagging in areas with Grizzlies or highly habituated black bears. Mama bears do teach the babies how to climb up to get rewards. As well, remember that mice, squirrels and birds will also attack silnylon food sacks.

More thoughts:

How you camp and eat can also play into whether or not you get night-time (even day time!) visitors.

Keep a clean camp. No crumbs, no washing dishes with food on them into the bushes. Don't leave open food in camp and wander off.

Avoid highly used campsites that bear the mark of bears if you can. Bears are smart and know what areas have sloppy campers. They do regular patrols of the easy areas, same with rodents and raccoons.

In Grizzly territory, stop an hour or two before camp and make your main meal. Eat and clean up and then continue hiking. This helps stop the smell association.

Maintain a kitchen area that is separate from your tent. Do not cook in your tent. Or eat in your tent.

Double-check your pack for wrappers before bed, same with your pants and jacket. Clean up before bed, wash your hands and face. In Grizzly territory you may be advised to sleep in clothing you do not cook in. Do consult the rangers about bear issues before setting out.

Hot & Cold Drinks

Sarah's Organic Hot Cocoa Master Mix

1 cup organic dry milk
1/4 cup organic cocoa powder
1/2 cup organic vanilla sugar (or make your own, it's easy!)
Pinch sea salt

Directions: Mix all ingredients together and store in an airtight container or bag.

Here are a few variations to the master recipe:

Spiced Hot Cocoa Mix

Add in to master mix:
1 tsp ground cardamom
1 tsp cinnamon
1 tsp ginger
1/2 tsp nutmeg

Mocha Mix

Add in to master mix:
2 Tbsp instant espresso powder

To prepare any of the versions: Add 1 cup boiling water to 1/4 cup dry mix. Stir till dissolved.

Makes about 7 servings

In Your Face Morning Mochas

1 1/4 cups instant milk
1 cup powdered sugar
1/2 cup cocoa powder
2 to 4 Tbsp instant espresso powder
1 tsp cornstarch
Pinch of salt

Mix together in a large bowl. Bag the powder into 1/2 cup portions. This should make about 6 servings.
2 Tbsp of espresso powder will provide a sweet mocha flavor, 4 Tbsp will give you the "bite" of a double shot.

Makes 5 to 6 servings

To prepare: Add 1 cup boiling water slowly to the mix, stirring well. Sip away and wake up!

Hot Eggnog for One

In a snack bag:
1/3 cup dry milk
1 Tbsp egg powder
1 tsp packed brown sugar
Dash each of ground cinnamon and nutmeg

Add 1 cup near boiling water to the dry ingredients. Stir well and serve.

Serves 1

Note: You can find egg powder online, such as Ova brand.

Warm Egg Nog

1 cup dry milk
1/4 cup egg powder
1/4 cup brown sugar
1/2 tsp ground cinnamon
1/4 tsp ground nutmeg

Mix everything together in a large bowl. Split equally into 5 zip top bags. This should be 1/3 cup of the dry mix per bag.
For each serving slowly add in 1 cup near boiling water and stir well.

Makes about 5 servings

Note: You can find egg powder online. Ova brand is one of our favorites.

Mocha Eggnog

In a snack bag:
1/3 cup dry milk
1 Tbsp egg powder
1 Tbsp malted milk powder
2 tsp instant cocoa mix
1 tsp instant coffee or espresso

Add 1 cup near boiling water to the dry ingredients. Stir well and serve.

Serves 1

Notes: You can find malted milk powder in the coffee/tea/cocoa aisle. Find egg powder online, such as Ova brand.

Spiced Cider Mix-in's

Add to a packet of commercial spiced cider:

1/4 tsp Dried Lemon or Orange Zest, stirred in.

1/4 tsp finely crumbled Dried Rosemary, let settle before drinking.

Brew a Chai flavored tea bag, stir in cider mix.

A caramel square in the bottom of your mug, stir in.

1 tsp Red Hots© or similar spicy cinnamon candies stirred in.

Trail Teas:

For the tea recipes, feel free to use whatever tea you like, be it black, green, white or any of the many herbal varieties.

If you have time in the morning you can brew up any tea mixture (herbal or otherwise), and let it steep in a quart bottle that is heat safe. When done steeping, cool the bottle off in a stream or lake. This can also be done in the evening, and allow it to chill overnight.

In the tea recipes where you are using loose herbs and or tea, we call for using cheesecloth or tea bags. This eliminates having to strain your tea before drinking. You can find in many natural food stores or online empty tea bags that you can fill yourself. Some are disposable; others are made of muslin fabric that you can reuse by rinsing out after use. You can also make your own tea bags economically by buying a box of unbleached coffee filters (the cone style, smallest size). Cut them down to size, fill up the bags, and use a sewing machine to seal the bag.

Rose Tea

1 Tbsp dried red rose petals

Also take:
1 Tbsp or 1 packet honey
1 packet True lemon or 1 packet lemon juice

Pour near boiling water over the petals; let steep for a couple of minutes. Add the lemon and honey.

Serves 1

Notes: You can dry rose petals quite easily in season; make sure they come from bushes not sprayed with chemicals! If using store bought, buy organic only and sold as food grade.

Mint Tea

Put into cheesecloth or a tea bag:
1 tsp dried mint
1 tsp loose leaf green tea

Also take:
1 Tbsp or 1 packet honey

Pour near boiling water over the tea and let steep till desired. Sweeten to taste.

Serves 1

Note: Mint tea is good if you have an upset stomach or indigestion after dinner.

Ginger tea

1 tsp powdered ginger
1 Tbsp or 1 packet honey

Bring 1 cup water to a boil. Pour over ginger and honey and let steep
for 5 minutes. Substitute diced crystallized (candied) ginger for a
different taste.

Serves 1

Note: Ginger tea is good if you are feeling nauseated, run down or
have stomach issues.

Spiced tea

At home combine:
1 1/2 tsp ground ginger
1 tsp ground cardamom
1/2 tsp ground cinnamon
1/2 tsp ground nutmeg
1/4 tsp ground cloves

Store in a small bag. Add 1/2 tsp or to taste to any cup of black or
green tea when steeping.

Makes about 8 servings

Sage Tea

1 teaspoon dried whole leaf sage
1 packet True Lemon or 1 packet lemon juice
1 Tbsp or 1 packet honey

Bring water to a boil. Pour over sage. Let steep for 5 minutes. Add lemon and honey to taste

Serves 1

Flowery Herbal Infusion

At home, combine:
1 Tbsp dried food grade lavender flowers
2 Tbsp dried peppermint
1 Tbsp dried summer savory
1 Tbsp dried sweet marjoram
1 Tbsp dried whole calendula flowers

Use 2 teaspoon per 12 ounce cup or separate into 9 zip top bags. Pour near boiling water over the herbs and let steep 3 to 5 minutes. Sweeten to taste.
Herbs can be put into tea bags or cheesecloth, if desired.

Makes 9 servings

Lavender Tea

1 tsp dried food grade lavender flowers
2 tsp dried mint leaves
1 Tbsp or 1 packet honey

Pour boiling water over the herbs; let steep for 5 minutes. The amount of water is up to your cup/mug size, 8 to 12 ounces. Strain, if desired, and serve hot. Sweeten to taste.

Serves 1

Note: This can also be made as iced tea, double the herbs and let steep in 1 quart of water.

Herbal Green Tea

1 tsp loose green tea leaves
1 tsp dried crumbled rosemary leaves
1/8 tsp ground nutmeg

Put all ingredients in a tea bag or cheesecloth and steep in near boiling water for 5 minutes. (8 to 12 ounce mug) Sweeten with honey, if desired, to taste.

Serves 1

Chai Tea

1 Chai flavor black tea bag
1 Tbsp dry milk
1 Tbsp or 1 packet honey

Pour boiling water over the tea bag and let steep till ready. Add in dry milk and honey to taste.

Serves 1

Hibiscus Tea

2 to 5 dried hibiscus flowers (find in ethnic and natural food stores)
Sugar or honey to taste

Place flowers in cup, cover with boiling water. Let steep till cool enough to drink. Sweeten if desired.

Serves 1

Note: This tea is good with dry milk added, producing a smooth tea, which is perfect for a nighttime drink. Stir in 1 to 2 Tablespoons dry milk before drinking.

Spicy Morning Tea

1/4 cup dried food grade lavender flowers
1/4 cup dried mint
1/4 cup dried rosemary leaves
2 Tbsp dried chamomile
2 Tbsp dried whole cloves

Combine all the ingredients. Store in a sealed bag or separate into 12 smaller bags.

Use 4 tsp of the mix per 12 ounces of boiling water, using cheesecloth or tea bag to hold tea. Let steep for 5 minutes. Sweeten to taste.

Makes 12 servings

Two Flower Tea

1 tsp dried food grade lavender flowers
1 tsp dried chamomile
1 tsp loose-leaf green tea

Combine in cheesecloth or tea bag.
To serve, cover with near boiling water and steep for 5 minutes.
Sweeten to taste.

Serves 1

Sun Tea:

Before you leave camp in the morning, fill a quart bottle with purified water and add your tea mixture. Clip it to your pack and as you walk during the day, your tea will brew. In camp tuck the bottle into a stream or lake to chill for dinner.

Sun Tea Lemonade

After brewing a quart of tea (herbal, black or green) add:
4 Tbsp lemon juice (1 large lemon)
2 Tbsp or 2 packets honey

Shake well.

Note:
If making at home before leaving for a hike, make a double batch of tea and freeze part of it as ice cubes, add to the drink before leaving, it will keep your drink cold and not get diluted tasting.

Flavors 1 quart

Trail Lemonade

In a quart water bottle:
4 packets True Lemon©, 2 Tbsp lemon juice or 1 small lemon
1 Tbsp or 1 packet honey

Combine the lemon juice and honey. Stir 1-cup cold water into it slowly.

Serves 1

Note: Use hot water for hot lemon toddy.

Maple Lemonade

In a quart water bottle:
8 packets True Lemon©, 1/4 cup lemon juice or 1 lemon
3 Tbsp pure maple syrup

Shake gently to combine. Add 1-quart cold filtered water. Put on cap tightly and shake for a minute.

Makes 1 quart

Maple Sugar Lemonade

In a quart water bottle:
8 packets True Lemon©, 1/4 cup lemon juice or 1 lemon
3 Tbsp maple sugar

Add 1-quart cold filtered water. Put on cap tightly and shake till sugar dissolves.

Makes 1 quart

Morning Shake

Pack in a quart bag:
1/3 cup dry milk
1 Tbsp yogurt powder
1 packet Instant Breakfast© mix, any flavor
2 Tbsp malt powder

Add one-cup cold water, seal tightly and shake for at least a minute. If near snow, stash in a snow bank for a few minutes to chill.

Serves 1

Notes: Instant breakfast, such as Carnation Breakfast Essentials, are found in the cereal or with hot cocoa. Yogurt powder is found online. Malt powder is found in the coffee/tea/cocoa aisle.

Nanner Smoothie

Pack in a quart bag:
1/3 cup dry milk
3 Tbsp malted milk powder
2 Tbsp freeze-dried banana powder

Add one-cup cold water, seal bag tightly and shake for at least a minute. If near snow, stash in a snow bank for a few minutes to chill.

Serves 1

Note: Find malted milk powder in the coffee/tea/cocoa aisle.

Breakfast Shake

In a sandwich bag:
1/3 cup dry milk
2 Tbsp dry creamer
1 Tbsp Bird's custard mix
1 packet instant breakfast, any flavor

Add 1 1/4 cups cold water to the bag, seal tightly and shake for a couple minutes or until fully mixed.

Serves 1

Notes: Find custard mix in the pudding aisle, often up high. Instant breakfast, such as Carnation Breakfast Essentials, are found in the cereal or with hot cocoa.

Cold Eggnog Shake

In a quart bag:
1/3 cup dry milk
3 Tbsp malted milk powder
2 Tbsp egg powder
1 Tbsp packed brown sugar
1/8 tsp ground cinnamon
Pinch of ground nutmeg
Pinch of salt

Add one-cup cold water, seal tightly and shake for at least a minute. If near snow, stash in a snow bank for a few minutes to chill.

Serves 1

Note: Find malted milk powder in the coffee/tea/cocoa aisle. Find egg powder online, such as Ova© brand.

Mocha Shake

In a quart freezer bag:
1/2 cup dry milk
1 Tbsp unsweetened cocoa powder
1 Tbsp sugar
1 tsp instant espresso or coffee

Add 1-cup cold water, seal tightly and shake till dissolved and frothed up. In an area with **clean** snow? Add a little in for an extra treat!

Serves 1

Breakfast Recipes

Cranberry Orange Cereal

In a sandwich bag:
1/2 cup + 2 Tbsp cornmeal
1/4 cup dried cranberries
1 Tbsp dried milk
1 tsp brown sugar
1/4 tsp cinnamon
1/4 tsp dried diced orange peel
Pinch salt
2 packets True® Orange© powder or 1 tsp orange drink mix

Bring 1 3/4 cups water to a boil. Lower the flame to low, add in the dry ingredients and stir well with a whisk for a couple minutes. Turn off the heat and let sit till cool enough to eat.

Serves 2

Maple Currant Cereal

In a sandwich bag:
1/2 cup + 2 Tbsp cornmeal
1 Tbsp maple sugar
1 Tbsp dried currants
1 Tbsp dry milk
1 tsp butter powder
Pinch salt

Bring 1 1/2 cups water to a boil. Turn the flame to low, add in the dry ingredients and stir well with a whisk for a couple minutes. Turn off the heat and let sit until cool enough to eat.

Serves 2

Notes: While dried currants are called for in this recipe, you can substitute your choice of dried or fresh fruit. My favorite is picking fresh huckleberries along the trail when in season. If you cannot find maple sugar, you can use maple syrup or brown sugar instead.

Apricots and Coconut Cream Cereal

In a sandwich bag:
1/2 cup + 2 Tbsp cornmeal
2 Tbsp sugar
2 Tbsp coconut cream powder
2 Tbsp diced dried apricots
1 tsp butter powder
Pinch kosher salt

Bring 1 1/2 cups water to a boil. Turn the flame down to low, add in the dry ingredients and stir well with a whisk for a couple minutes. Turn off the heat and let sit until cool enough to eat.

Serves 2

Pears and Vanilla Oatmeal

In a quart or pint freezer bag:
2 packets plain instant oatmeal
2 Tbsp freeze dried or dehydrated pears, diced
1 tsp vanilla powder
1 tsp maple sugar

FBC method: Add 1 cup near boiling water slowly to the freezer bag, stir well and let sit for a couple minutes to cool.

Insulated mug method: Add 1 cup boiling water slowly and stir well and let sit for a couple minutes to cool.

One pot method: Bring 1 cup water to boil in your pot. Turn the stove off and add in the dry ingredients. Stir well and let sit for a couple minutes to cool.

Serves 1

Eggnog Oatmeal

In a quart freezer or sandwich bag:
2 packets plain or brown sugar instant oatmeal
1/3 cup eggnog drink mix
2 Tbsp dried golden raisins

FBC method: Add 1 cup near boiling water to the dry ingredients and stir well. Let sit covered for 5 minutes.

Insulated mug method: Add 1 cup near boiling water to the dry ingredients and stir well. Cover loosely and let sit for 5 minutes.

One pot method: Bring 1 cup water to a boil in your pot. Turn off the stove, add in the dry ingredients and stir well. Let sit till cool enough to eat.

Serves 1

Note: See the Drinks Section for the eggnog drink mix recipe.

Trail Mix Couscous Cereal

In a sandwich bag:
1/2 cup whole wheat couscous
3 Tbsp diced dried fruit (whatever you like)
3 Tbsp dry milk
3/4 tsp ground cinnamon
1/4 tsp salt

In a small bag:
2 Tbsp finely chopped almonds
2 Tbsp flaked coconut

Also take:
2 Tbsp or 2 packets honey

In a pot, bring 3/4 cup of water and half of the honey to a boil. Remove pot from the stove and add the contents of the sandwich bag to the mixture; stirring well to combine. Cover tightly and let sit for 10 minutes. Stir again, then top with the nuts/coconut mix and the remaining honey drizzled over. Enjoy.

Serves 2

Coconut Fruit Rice

In a sandwich bag:
1 1/2 cups instant rice
1/2 tsp cinnamon
2 Tbsp coconut cream powder
1 Tbsp shredded coconut
1 Tbsp diced walnuts
1 Tbsp brown sugar
Pinch of salt

In a sandwich bag:
1/4 cup diced dried fruit of choice

Also take:
2 Tbsp butter
1 packet honey

Cover the dried fruit with water and let sit for 10 minutes. Drain well, reserving water.
At the same time, melt the butter over medium flame in your pot. Add in the fruit and let sauté for a minute.
Add water to the reserved soaking water, to make 1 1/2 cups, add to the pot and bring to a boil. Add the dry ingredients and stir well. Turn off the stove and let sit for 10 minutes in a pot cozy. Fluff with fork and drizzle the honey.

Serves 2

Sunrise Rice Pudding

In a sandwich bag:
1 cup instant rice
4 ounce package instant vanilla pudding
1/2 cup freeze-dried oranges
2 Tbsp dry milk
1/4 tsp ground cinnamon
1/8 tsp dried orange zest

Bring 1 3/4 cups water to a boil in your pot. Add in the dry ingredients; turn the flame down to low. Simmer for a minute, stirring well. Take off the stove, cover tightly and let sit for 10 minutes. In cool temperatures use a pot cozy. If thin, put the pot back on your flame for a few seconds and it will thicken nicely.

Serves 2

Breakfast Bulgur Porridge

In a sandwich bag:
1/2 cup medium-grind bulgur
1/3 cup dry milk
1/4 cup raisins
1/4 tsp salt
2 Tbsp brown sugar
1/4 cup freeze-dried sliced strawberries

In your pot, bring to boil 2 cups water. Add in the dry ingredients to the pot, stirring well. Turn the flame to low and simmer for 5 minutes. Turn off the heat, cover tightly and let sit for 10 minutes. In cold temperatures, place the pot in a pot cozy to keep it warm.

Serves 2

Sausage Grits

In a quart freezer bag:
2 packets instant grits
1 Tbsp butter powder
1 tbsp shelf stable Parmesan cheese
1 tsp diced dried onions
1/4 tsp ground black pepper

Also take:
1 stick shelf stable sausage

FBC method: Dice the sausage up. Meanwhile, bring 1 cup water to a near boil. Add the sausage in the bag along with the water. Stir well, seal tightly and let sit for 5 minutes.

Insulated mug method: Dice the sausage up. Meanwhile, bring to a boil 1 cup water. Add the sausage and water to the dry ingredients and stir well. Cover tightly and let sit for 5 minutes.

One pot method: Dice the sausage up. In your pot bring 1 cup water to a boil. Add in the sausage and dry ingredients and stir well. Turn off the stove and cover tightly, letting sit for 5 minutes.

Serves 1

Chocolate Peanut Butter Oatmeal

In a sandwich or pint freezer bag:
2 packs plain instant oatmeal
1 packet hot cocoa mix (your choice)
1 Tbsp peanut butter

FBC method: Add the peanut butter to the dry ingredients with 1 cup near boiling water. Stir well and let sit till cool enough to eat.

Insulated mug method: Add the peanut butter to the dry ingredients with 1 cup boiling water. Stir well and let sit till cool enough to eat.

One pot method: Bring 1 cup water to a boil in your pot. Turn off the stove, add in the dry ingredients and stir well. Let sit till cool enough to eat.

Serves 1

Note: You can always use a serving of one of the hot cocoa mixes found in the hot drinks section.

Blueberry and Lemon Oatmeal

In a sandwich or pint freezer bag:
2 packets instant plain oatmeal
1 tsp dried lemon zest
1/4 cup dried blueberries
1 Tbsp brown sugar
1 tsp vanilla powder

Also take 1 packet honey (1 Tbsp)

FBC method: Add honey and 1 cup near boiling water to the dry ingredients. Stir well and add more water as needed till smooth. Let sit till cool enough to eat.

Insulated mug method: Add honey and 1 cup boiling water to the dry ingredients. Stir well and add more water as needed till smooth. Let sit till cool enough to eat.

One pot method: Bring 1 cup water to a boil in your pot. Turn off the stove, add in the homey and dry ingredients and stir well. Let sit till cool enough to eat.

Serves 1

Lazy Morning Oatmeal

In a sandwich bag:
2 cups quick cooking oats (not instant)

In a sandwich bag:
3/4 cup freeze-dried or dried apricots
2 Tbsp shredded coconut
1/3 cup dry milk
2 Tbsp honey powder

Bring 5 cups water and the apricot bag ingredients to a boil in your pot. Add in the oats, return to a boil and simmer on lowered heat for 1 minute or till the thickness you like. Let sit and cool.

Serves 2 to 3

Notes: Add more sweeteners as desired. For more coconut flavor, use coconut cream powder for the dry milk.

Instant Oatmeal Packets

This is an open-ended recipe "base" and you can make as many packets as you would like with it!

Ingredients:
Old-fashioned oats
Quick cooking oats
Salt

Put 1/2 cup old-fashioned oats at a time in a blender or mini food processor and blend on high until broken apart and somewhat powdery. Set aside in a small bowl, and repeat procedure if you are making a bigger batch.

In each pint size freezer bag put:
1/4 cup quick cooking oats
2 Tbsp powdered oats
1 Tbsp dry milk, soy or rice milk powder or coconut cream powder
1/8 tsp kosher salt (if desired)

FBC method:
Add 3/4 cup near boiling water. Stir, seal tightly and put in a cozy for 5 minutes.

One pot method:
Bring 3/4 cup water to a boil, take off the heat and add in the dry ingredients. Stir well, cover tightly and let sit for a couple minutes.

Variations:

Apple Cinnamon Oatmeal:
1 Tbsp sugar, 1/4 tsp cinnamon and 2 Tbsp diced dried apples.

Sweetened Oatmeal:
1 Tbsp sugar.

Brown Sugar and Cinnamon Oatmeal:
1 Tbsp brown sugar and 1/4 tsp cinnamon.

Raisins and Brown Sugar Oatmeal:
1 Tbsp packed brown sugar and 1 Tbsp raisins.

Hippy Oatmeal:
2 Tbsp wheat germ and 1 Tbsp diced toasted pecans.

Peaches and Cream Oatmeal:
1 Tbsp full fat dry milk and 2 Tbsp diced dried peaches.

Confetti Oatmeal:
1 tsp decorative cake/cookie sprinkles.

S'More Oatmeal:
6 miniature marshmallows and 1 Tbsp chocolate chips.

Cookies and Cream Oatmeal:
1 crushed chocolate stuffed cookie and 1 Tbsp full fat dry milk.

Walnut and Quinoa Granola

1/2 cup raw quinoa
1/2 cup rolled oats
2 Tbsp diced walnuts
1/8 tsp kosher salt
2 Tbsp honey or maple syrup
2 Tbsp raisins or dried cranberries

At home:
Preheat your oven to 225*. Rinse the quinoa and shake dry. In a medium pot add the quinoa and cover with water. Bring to a boil and cook for 7 minutes. Take off the stove, drain and rinse with cold water. Combine everything but the raisins on an ungreased cookie sheet and place in the oven. Check every 10 minutes and stir often with a silicone spatula so it toasts evenly. Cook until dry and lightly toasted, about 45 minutes. Mix in the raisins and let cool. Once cool store in an airtight container or plastic storage bag.

For trail:
Pack how much granola you like to eat in a sandwich bag. To serve sprinkle 1/3 cup dry milk powder or 2 Tbsp soy milk powder in the bag along with 1 cup water. Stir well and serve.

Servings depend on appetite

Hippy Muesli

1 cup rolled oats
1/2 cup raisins or dried cranberries
1/4 cup diced walnuts
1/4 cup toasted wheat germ
1/4 cup wheat bran
1/4 cup toasted shelled sunflower seeds
2 Tbsp ground flaxseed
1 tsp cinnamon
1/2 tsp dried diced orange peel

At home:
Mix everything together well. Store in an airtight container or plastic storage bag.

On trail:
Pack how much cereal you like to eat in a sandwich bag. To serve sprinkle 1/3 cup dry milk powder or 2 Tbsp soy milk powder in the bag plus 1 cup of cool water. Stir well and serve.

Servings depend on appetite

Breakfast Energy Bars

1 cup honey or agave nectar
1 cup sugar
1 tsp salt
1 tsp pure vanilla extract
1 cup crunchy peanut butter
1 box cereal (15 to 18 ounces, berry/nut/flake type)

In a large microwave-safe bowl heat the honey, sugar and salt to a boil. Carefully remove and stir in to the mixture the vanilla and peanut butter until smooth. Add in the cereal and toss quickly to coat.

At this point you can pack the mixture into a greased 13"x9" pan, cutting into bars when cool or you can roll balls of it with your hands for a quick bite. Store in a tightly sealed plastic bag.

Servings depend on size cut.

Peanut Butter Granola Bites

1/4 cup honey
1/4 cup creamy peanut butter
1 cup puffed wheat or rice cereal
3/4 cup granola of choice

Grease a 9" x 5" loaf pan with butter or cooking spray and set aside.

In a large saucepan heat the honey over medium heat till it comes to a boil. Pull off the heat and stir in the peanut butter. Quickly work the cereals in till coated. Using a silicone spatula pack the mixture into the pan. Chill in the refrigerator for a couple hours, turn out of the pan and cut into pieces. Stash in the refrigerator until trip time. Cary tightly sealed in a plastic bag.

Servings depend on the size you cut.

Fry Pan Recipes

For best results, use a slick nonstick fry pan or fry pan lid, or a wide/shallow 2 Liter cooking pot. Use plenty of oil, keep the flame low on your stove and don't turn away while things are sizzling.

Base DIY Biscuit Mix

1 1/8 cups all-purpose flour
1 Tbsp baking powder
1 1/2 tsp sugar
1/4 tsp salt
3 Tbsp vegetable oil

In a large bowl mix together the dry ingredients; slowly drizzle in the oil while mixing in with a fork. Finish blending in with your fingers till the oil is fully incorporated. Makes a shy 2 cups base mix. Use in place of commercial all-in-one biscuit mix.

To use:
1 cup mix + 1/3 cup water will serve 2, pack mix in a zip top sandwich bag. Add water to bag, seal tightly and knead gently till mixed. Heat a non-stick pot over medium heat, add in one Tablespoon oil, and heat up. Add the dough into the pot, cover with the pot's lid and lower the heat to a low flame. Cook 5 minutes then drizzle another Tablespoon of oil on the dough. Flip and cook 5 more minutes or until firm to the touch. Keep an eye on it while baking, using a mini spatula to check under for getting too brown.

When they are golden brown turn off the stove.

Serves 1 to 2

Note: In all the recipes for "baking" keep any eye on your treats. You many need to adjust the flame or hold the fry pan an inch above the flame. You can also use a heat diffuser, a small metal tool that weighs around 3 to 4 ounces, which will prevent most scorching in both fry pans and thin pots.

Easy Trail Pancakes

In a sandwich bag:
1 cup biscuit mix
1/3 cup dry milk

Also take:
1 to 2 Tbsp or 1 to 2 packets vegetable oil

Add 1 1/4 cups water to the bag, seal tightly and knead /shake bag till combined into pancake batter. Coat your fry pan with oil and heat over medium flame. Cut off a bottom corner of the bag and squeeze 4-inch circles of batter into the pan. (If you have ever used a piping bag for frosting, it is kind like this) Cook 2 minutes or until bubbles form on top of the pancake. Flip with a spatula and cook another 1 minute or until pancakes are golden brown. Repeat until you have used all of the batter.

You may need to lower the stove's heat and /or keep the fry pan above the flame to prevent scorching.

Makes about 7 pancakes, serves 1 to 2 depending on how hungry you are.

Variations:

Ginger Maple Pancakes
Add 1 Tablespoon diced crystallized (candied) ginger and 2 Tablespoons maple sugar to mix.

Chocolate Peanut Butter Pancakes
Sprinkle a few mini chocolate chips on top of each pancake after pouring. Serve with creamy peanut butter and maple syrup on top.

Savory Bacon Chive Pancake
Add in 2 Tablespoons shelf stable bacon or 'bacon' TVP and 1 Tablespoon dried chives to mix. Top with pepper or sausage gravy on top or drizzle maple syrup and more shelf stable bacon on.

Basic DIY Pancakes

In a sandwich bag:
1 cup all-purpose flour
1 tsp baking powder
1/3 cup dry milk
1/4 tsp salt

Also take:
2 Tbsp vegetable oil

Add 1-cup water and 1 tablespoon oil to the bag. Seal tightly and knead/shake bag until combined into pancake batter. Coat your fry pan with remaining vegetable oil and heat over medium flame. Cut off a bottom corner of the bag and squeeze 4-inch circles of batter into the pan. (If you have ever used a piping bag for frosting, it is kind like this) Cook 2 minutes or until bubbles form on top of the pancake. Flip with a spatula and cook another 1 minute or until pancakes are golden brown. Repeat until you have used all of the batter.

You may need to lower the stove's heat and /or keep the fry pan above the flame to prevent scorching.

Serves 1 to 2

Huckleberry Pancakes

In a sandwich bag:
1 cup all-purpose flour
1 tsp baking powder
1/3 cup dry milk
1/4 tsp salt

Also take:
2 Tbsp or 2 packets vegetable oil

On the trail: pick two small handfuls of wild huckleberries or blueberries (about ½ cup total).

Add 1-cup water and 1 Tablespoon oil to the bag. Seal tightly and knead/shake bag until combined; stir in huckleberries. Coat your fry pan with oil and heat over medium flame. Cut a corner off your bag and squeeze 4-inch circles of batter into pan. Cook 2 minutes or until bubbles form on top. Flip with a spatula and cook 1 minute more or until pancakes are golden brown. Repeat till done.

You may need to lower the stove's heat and /or keep the fry pan above the flame to prevent scorching.

Serves 1 to 2

Notes: To use dried blueberries instead of fresh berries, pack the dried berries in a small bag. Then add 1/2 cup of water to the bag and let rehydrate for 5 minutes. Make the batter using 1 1/2 cups water, and then add the berries and water.

Maple Citrusy Huckleberry Sauce

In a small bag:
1 packet True Lemon powder or 1 packet lemon juice
1 Tbsp brown sugar

Also take:
1/2 cup maple syrup in a leak proof bottle
1 Tbsp butter

Pick on the trail: 1/2 pint wild huckleberries or blueberries.

This is perfect to whip up in a titanium or stainless steel mug on the stove.

Melt the butter over low heat and add the huckleberries. Mash some of the berries with your spork. Add the other items and simmer over low heat for about 5 minutes until the mixture starts to thicken.

Makes about 1 cup syrup

Peanut Butter Banana Pancakes

In a sandwich bag:
1 cup biscuit mix
1/3 cup dry milk
1/4 cup freeze-dried bananas, crushed
1/4 teaspoon ground cinnamon

Also take:
1 single serving packet or 2 Tbsp peanut butter
2 Tbsp or 2 packets vegetable oil

Add 1 1/4 cups water and the peanut butter to the bag. Seal tightly and knead/shake bag till combined.

Coat your fry pan with oil and heat over medium flame. Cut a corner off your bag and squeeze 4-inch circles of batter into pan. Cook 2 minutes or until bubbles form on top. Flip with a spatula and cook 1 minute more or until pancakes are golden brown. Repeat till done.

You may need to lower the stove's heat and /or keep the fry pan above the flame to prevent scorching.

Serves 1 to 2

Oatmeal Pancakes

Pack in a quart freezer bag:
1 cup uncooked rolled oats

Pack in a second sandwich bag:
1/3 cup dry milk
1/2 cup all purpose flour
2 tsp baking powder
1/4 cup powdered eggs

Also take 1/4 cup oil in a leak-proof bottle or 4 packets oil.

Combine oats, 2 Tablespoons oil and 2 cups of water in the freezer bag, mash up and let sit for 10 minutes. Stir in dry ingredients till you have a batter.

Coat your fry pan with oil and heat over medium flame. Cut a corner off your bag and squeeze 4-inch circles of batter into pan. Cook 2 minutes or until bubbles form on top. Flip with a spatula and cook 1 minute more or until pancakes are golden brown. Repeat till done.

You may need to lower the stove's heat and /or keep the fry pan above the flame to prevent scorching.

Serves 1 to 2

Pecan Pancakes

Pack in a quart freezer bag:
1 1/4 cups all-purpose flour
1/4 cup diced toasted pecans
2 Tbsp sugar
2 tsp baking powder
1/2 tsp salt

Also pack 2 Tbsp or 2 packets oil

Add 1 1/3 cups water; stir well till you have a batter.

Coat your fry pan with oil and heat over medium flame. Cut a corner off your bag and squeeze 4-inch circles of batter into pan. Cook 2 minutes or until bubbles form on top. Flip with a spatula and cook 1 minute more or until pancakes are golden brown. Repeat till done.

You may need to lower the stove's heat and /or keep the fry pan above the flame to prevent scorching.

Serves 1 to 2

Gingerbread Pancakes with Brown Sugar Syrup

In a gallon freezer bag:
2 cups flour
3/4 cup baking mix (commercial or homemade)
1/4 cup sugar
1 Tbsp ground ginger
1 Tbsp instant coffee or espresso powder
4 tsp baking powder
2 tsp ground cinnamon
1/2 tsp salt

Add 3 cups water, seal tightly and shake to combine, making sure the corners are mixed.

Coat your fry pan with oil and heat over medium flame. Cut a corner off your bag and squeeze 4-inch circles of batter into pan. Cook 2 minutes or until bubbles form on top. Flip with a spatula and cook 1 minute more or until pancakes are golden brown. Repeat till done.

You may need to lower the stove's heat and /or keep the fry pan above the flame to prevent scorching.

Brown Sugar Syrup

In a sandwich bag:
1/2 cup dark brown sugar

Add 1/2 cup water, seal the bag and shake till mixed. Let sit while you prepare the pancakes.

Serves 2 to 4, depending on appetite

Pancake Fruit and Cream Burritos

What to do with leftovers? Make morning snacks!

Stack of leftover pancakes
Cream cheese packets
Jam or jelly packets
Fresh berries (if lucky!)

If you are lucky enough to have leftovers after breakfast let them cool
and stash in a clean sandwich bag till snack time.
Spread cream cheese, top with jam or jelly, sprinkle on any found wild
berries (of the eating type) and roll up burrito style.

Fruit Scones

In a quart bag:
1 cup all-purpose flour
1/4 cup sugar
1/4 cup buttermilk powder
1/4 cup dried blueberries
1/4 cup diced dried cherries
2 tsp baking powder
1/4 tsp cinnamon
1/4 tsp salt

Also take:
1/4 cup butter in a small bag
2 Tbsp or 2 packets oil

Add butter to the bag, pushing out any air and seal tightly. Knead the bag with your fingers until mixture is crumbly. This can be done at home before you leave, if desired, on shorter trips.

Add 1/4 cup cool water to the bag, seal tightly again and keep kneading until dough forms. Take the dough out and pat into a disk about 1/2 inch thick. (Or do it through the bag to keep hands clean.) Heat a non-stick pot over medium heat. Add in one Tablespoon oil, and heat up. Add in the circle of dough. Cover with the pots lid and lower the heat to a low flame. Cook 5 minutes then drizzle the other Tablespoon of oil on the dough. Flip and cook 5 more minutes or until firm to the touch. Keep an eye on it while baking, using a mini spatula to check under for getting too brown. During the baking you may need to lower the heat or raise the pan off the stove a bit and hold it above the flame. When they are golden brown turn off the stove.

Note: Find buttermilk powder with the dry milk in grocery stores or in the baking aisle. You can use shortening for the butter if on long trips or substitute Ghee butter, which is perfect for long trips.

Cheddar Bacon Biscuits

In a quart bag:
3/4 cup biscuit mix
2 Tbsp 'bacon' TVP bits or shelf stable bacon pieces
1 tsp dried chives
1/4 tsp ground black pepper
1/4 tsp dried garlic

Also take:
2 ounce cheddar cheese
2 Tbsp or 2 packets oil

Dice the cheese and add to the bag. Mix in 1/4 cup cool water with a long handled spoon. Knead the dough through the bag. The dough will be stiff. If you can, pat it out like a pizza shell between your hands. Heat a non-stick pot over medium heat. Add in one Tablespoon oil, and heat up. Add the circle of dough into the pot. Cover with the pots lid and lower the heat to a low flame. Cook 5 minutes then drizzle the other tablespoon of oil on the dough. Flip and cook 5 more minutes or until firm to the touch. Keep an eye on it while baking, using a mini spatula to check under for getting too brown. During the baking you may need to lower the heat or raise the pan off the stove a bit and hold it above the flame. When they are golden brown turn off the stove.

Serves 1 to 2

Ginger Cinnamon Scones

In a quart bag:
3/4 cup biscuit mix
3 Tbsp sugar
2 Tbsp coconut cream powder
1 Tbsp diced candied ginger
1/2 tsp ground cinnamon

Also take 2 Tbsp or 2 packets oil

Add in 1/4 cup cool water to the bag. Seal the bag tightly and knead the dough through the bag. The dough may be sticky. Heat a non-stick pot over medium heat. Add in one-tablespoon oil and heat up. Using your spoon, drop the dough into your pot. Cover with the pots lid and lower the heat to a low flame. Cook 5 minutes then drizzle the other tablespoon of oil on the dough. Flip and cook 5 more minutes or until firm to the touch. Keep an eye on it while baking, using a mini spatula to check under for getting too brown. During the baking you may need to lower the heat or raise the pan off the stove a bit and hold it above the flame. When they are golden brown turn off the stove.

Serves 1 to 2

Oatmeal and Cranberry Biscuits

In a sandwich bag:
1 cup biscuit mix
1/4 cup quick cooking oats
2 Tbsp dry milk
2 Tbsp dried sweetened cranberries
1 Tbsp honey powder

Also take 2 Tbsp or 2 packets oil

Add 1/2 cup cool water to the bag. Seal the bag tightly and knead the dough through the bag. Heat a non-stick pot over medium heat. Add in one-tablespoon oil and heat up. Add the dough into the pot. Cover with the pots lid and lower the heat to a low flame. Cook 5 minutes then drizzle the other tablespoon of oil on the dough. Flip and cook 5 more minutes or until firm to the touch. Keep an eye on it while baking, using a mini spatula to check under for getting too brown. During the baking you may need to lower the heat or raise the pan off the stove a bit and hold it above the flame. When they are golden brown turn off the stove.

Serves 1 to 2

Eggnog Coconut Biscuits

In a sandwich bag:
1 cup biscuit mix
1/3 up dry eggnog mix
1/4 cup natural shredded coconut
3 Tbsp coconut cream powder

Also take 2 Tbsp or 2 packets oil

Add 1/2 cup cool water to the bag. Seal the bag tightly and knead the dough through the bag. Heat a non-stick pot over medium heat. Add in one-tablespoon oil and heat up. Add the dough into the pot. Cover with the pots lid and lower the heat to a low flame. Cook 5 minutes then drizzle the other tablespoon of oil on the dough. Flip and cook 5 more minutes or until firm to the touch. Keep an eye on it while baking, using a mini spatula to check under for getting too brown. During the baking you may need to lower the heat or raise the pan off the stove a bit and hold it above the flame. When they are golden brown turn off the stove.

Serves 1 to 2

Note: Find the eggnog drink mix in the hot drinks section.

Spiced Breakfast Fry Bread

Pack in a quart freezer bag:
1 1/2 cups all-purpose flour
2 Tbsp sugar
1 1/2 tsp baking powder
1 tsp ground cinnamon
1/8 tsp salt
1/4 cup diced roasted pecans
1/4 cup raisins or dried cranberries

Also pack 2 Tbsp or 2 packets oil

Slowly add water, starting with 1 cup up to 1 1/2 cups, to the bag till you get a thick batter. Stir or knead the bag gently.
Add to your pot or fry pan 1 Tablespoon oil and heat over a low flame. Add in the batter and cook for 10 minutes, checking to avoid burning, lowering the flame if needed. When browned, drizzle the second Tablespoon oil on top and flip over carefully, bake until browned on other side, between 5 and 10 minutes.

Serves 2 to 3, depending on appetite

Sausage and Hash Browns Skillet

In a sandwich bag:
1 cup dried hash browns
3 Tbsp freeze-dried sausage or sausage TVP
1 Tbsp diced dried bell peppers
1 tbsp diced dried onion
1/2 tsp diced dried garlic
1/4 tsp ground black pepper

In a small bag:
3 eggs worth of commercial dried eggs
(Mark on bag how much water to rehydrate according to package)

Also take:
1 packet or Tbsp oil
2 ounces cheddar cheese

Add 1 1/4 cups cool water to the hash browns bag. Seal tightly and let sit for at least 30 minutes to rehydrate. Meanwhile add water called for to the egg bag. Seal tightly and shake to dissolve. Dice up the cheese. Heat the oil up in your pot; add in the hash browns mix and cook, stirring constantly till browned. Make a hole in the center, add in the egg mixture and start scrambling, tossing the eggs through the hash browns. Once cooked, take off the heat and mix in the cheese.

Serves 2 to 3

Hash Brown Skillet

In a quart freezer bag:
1 cup instant hash browns
1/4 cup commercial dried eggs
2 Tbsp shelf stable bacon or bacon bits
2 Tbsp dry milk
1 1/2 tsp all-purpose flour
1 tsp diced dried onion
1 tsp dried bell pepper
1/2 tsp dried parsley
1/4 tsp ground black pepper

Also take:
1 Tbsp or 1 packet oil

Add 1 1/4 cups water to the bag, seal tightly and put in a cozy for 15 to 30 minutes. Heat the oil in a shallow pot or fry pan lid over a medium flame. Add the potato mixture and cook till browned, flip over and brown the other side.

Serves 1

Spicy Hash Browns

In a quart freezer bag:
1 1/4 cups instant hash browns
2 Tbsp diced dried bell peppers
1/4 to 1/2 tsp diced dried jalapeños
1 tsp onion powder
1/2 tsp granulated garlic
1/2 tsp ground cumin
1/2 tsp ground coriander
1/4 tsp salt
1/4 tsp ground black pepper

Also take 2 Tbsp or 2 packets oil

Add 1 1/2 cups very warm water to the bag, seal tightly and let sit in a cozy for at least 30 minutes to rehydrate.
Heat the oil in a wide 2-liter pot over a medium flame, add in the hash browns and cook till crispy and golden brown, stirring as needed.
Serve with ketchup if desired.

Serves 2

Notes: Dried jalapeños have quite the kick, so use the lower end if you do not like as much heat. To make more filling consider adding in 1/2 cup freeze-dried sausage withe the hash browns. Add an additional 1/2 cup water and let rehydrate as noted.

Scrambled Eggs

In a snack size bag:
1/4 cup crumbled dried mushrooms

In a sandwich bag:
1/2 cup commercially dried eggs
1 Tbsp dry milk
1 Tbsp butter powder
1 tsp dry parsley
1/2 tsp diced dried garlic
Salt and pepper to taste, if desired

Also take 1 Tbsp or 1 packet oil

Add 1/4 cup cool water to the mushroom bag, seal tightly and let sit for 30 minutes. Drain off any remaining water.
Heat the oil over a low flame in a non-stick wide pot or fry pan lid and sauté them for a couple minutes.
Meanwhile, add 1-cup cool water to the egg bag, seal tightly and shake for a couple minutes. Let sit for 10 to 15 minutes for the eggs to rehydrate properly.
When the mushrooms are smelling good, pour in the egg mixture and scramble gently till cooked to your preference. Season to taste and serve.

Serves 1

Notes: Read your dried egg's packaging for the amount of water needed to rehydrate. Ours called for 1/4 cup water for every 2 Tbsp of egg powder to equal 1 egg. Your chosen brand may vary! You will want 4 eggs worth for the recipe.

Leftover Oatmeal Cakes

So lets say you make up oatmeal and either you made too much or no one wants it, what to do with it? Fry it up!

Leftover cooked oatmeal, cooled
Vegetable oil, coconut oil or butter
Maple syrup
Cream cheese packets
Jam or Jelly packets

Before moving on for the day take the cold oatmeal and cut or scoop out into portions. In a fry pan lid, heat up a Tablespoon of oil over a low flame. Drop the oatmeal in and fry till golden brown, flipping over once.

Serve with syrup, or spread cream cheese and jam on top.

Makes as many as the leftovers you have!

Lunches

Trail Quesadillas

Take with you:
2 soft taco size soft tortillas
1 ounce cheese of choice

Using the lid of your pan, carefully heat it over your stove till warm (low heat). Lay one tortilla on the lid, thinly slice the cheese and lay it on the tortilla. Top with the other tortilla. Holding the pan over your stove, cook till starting to melt and getting golden brown then carefully flip to the other side and heat till it smells perfect. Eat greedily and don't share.

If your stove is a hot burning one, you may have to hold the lid just above the stove, so your tortillas do not burn.

Option: Add a couple packets of salsa on top of the cheese before heating.

Serves 1.

Spicy Chicken Quesadillas and Mexi Rice

Take:
7 ounce pouch chicken breast
2 ounces pepper jack cheese
4 soft taco size flour tortillas
2 large packets or 4 small packets salsa

Open chicken pouch and flake chicken. Mix in salsa and cheese, diced up. Spread mixture on 2 tortillas. Top with remaining tortillas.

Place 1 tortilla in your fry pan or pot over low heat. Brown tortilla on one until side crispy then flip and do the same on other side. Serve with the rice, recipe below.

Serves 2

Mexi Rice:

In a quart freezer bag put:
1 cup instant rice
1/4 cup dehydrated Pico de Gallo mix

FBC Method: Add 1 1/4 cups near boiling water. Stir, seal tightly and put in a cozy for 15 minutes. Fluff up. Serve with quesadillas or burritos.

Serves 2 as a side dish

Note: Find the Pico de Gallo recipe in the dry mixes and seasoning section.

Lentil Burritos

In a quart freezer bag:
3/4 cup cooked and dehydrated lentils
1/4 cup instant rice
1 Tbsp toasted sesame seeds
1/4 tsp kosher salt
1/8 tsp cumin
1/8 tsp mild curry powder
1/8 tsp cayenne pepper

Also take:
2 burrito size or 4 soft taco size tortillas
Salsa packets

FBC method: Add 1 cup near boiling water to the bag, seal tightly and let sit for 15 minutes. Fill tortillas and top with salsa.

One pot method: Bring 1 cup water to a boil, add in the dry ingredients. Stir and cover tightly, let sit for 15 minutes. Fill tortillas and top with salsa.

Serves 2

Note: Add in diced cheddar cheese if desired. This can also be paired with the mexi rice recipe elsewhere in this book.

Bagel Pizzas

Take in a snack bag:
1/2 cup diced sun-dried tomatoes

Also take:
2 bagels
1 small pouch pizza sauce (under 3 ounces)
2 pieces string cheese (2 ounces)
1 Tbsp or 1 packet vegetable oil

Cover the tomatoes with cool water and let sit for 15 minutes. Dice the cheese.

Heat your pot over medium heat. Add a small amount of oil. Lower the heat to low. Meanwhile, spread the sauce on the bagels, place in pan. Drain the tomatoes and top with them and cheese. Cover the pot with its lid, to allow cheese to melt.

Serves 2.

Notes: Add whatever toppings you like, from pepperoni and summer sausage to dried vegetables that you have rehydrated before hand with the tomatoes. You may need to do this in batches of two bagel halves if you have a small pot.

Lemon Olive Tuna Wraps

In a small bag:
2 Tbsp freeze-dried olives
1/2 tsp True Lemon© powder (2 packets) or 2 packets lemon juice
1/4 tsp dried lemon peel
1/4 tsp ground black pepper

Also take:
3 ounce package albacore tuna
1 Tbsp or 1 packet olive oil
1 large or 2 small flour tortillas

In a small zip top bag:
1 tsp capers

Add two Tablespoons cool water and oil to the olive bag. Seal tightly and let sit for 15 minutes. Open the tuna bag and smash up the fish. Mix in the olives (and capers) into the pouch. Serve on tortillas.

Serves 1

Note: Capers are pickled so carry well for a couple days tightly sealed. Be sure to pack them with some of the brine. They can also be dehydrated beforehand, soak in water for 15 minutes before using.

First Day Out Spinach and Artichoke Wrap

15 ounce can artichoke hearts packed in water, well drained
2 whole-wheat sandwich wraps or burrito size flour tortillas
4 slices provolone cheese
1 red bell pepper, ribs and seeds removed, cut into strips
1 cup fresh baby spinach
Coarse salt and ground pepper, if desired

At home wrap artichoke hearts in paper towels; squeeze out liquid and coarsely chop.
Set wraps or tortillas on counter. Lay 2 cheese slices down center of each. Divide evenly between wraps the artichoke, bell pepper, and spinach on top of cheese. Season with salt and pepper if desired. Fold in tops and bottoms of wraps by about 1 inch, then roll tightly from one of the open sides to enclose filling. Wrap tightly in plastic or waxed paper. Store in frig and carry in a cooler to the trailhead. Eat for lunch first day out.

Serves 2

Notes: These prepare well the night before, so you can grab and go to get on the trail. You can use marinated packed in oil artichokes, drain well. They will add a bit more flavor. You can also brush your wraps with the flavored oil before laying down the cheese for a great taste.

First Day Out Chicken Salad and Havarti Cheese Wrap

Take:
7 ounce pouch chicken
2 packets mayonnaise
1 packet Dijon mustard

In a small bag:
1 Tbsp diced dried shallot
1/4 teaspoon dried thyme leaves

Also take:
2 spinach-flavored sandwich wraps or burrito sized flour tortillas
4 slices Havarti cheese

Pack in a sandwich bag:
1 cup fresh baby spinach

Open the chicken pouch; add in the mayonnaise, mustard, shallot and Thyme. Mix together well, using a long handled spoon and let sit for a few minutes to meld flavors.

Lay the wraps on paper towels. Leaving a 1-inch border all around, layer the cheese, spinach and chicken mixture.

Fold in tops and bottoms of wraps by about 1 inch, then roll tightly from one of the open sides to enclose filling. Wrap tightly in plastic or waxed paper. Store in frig and carry in a cooler to the trailhead. Eat for lunch first day out.

Serves 2

First Day Out Hummus and Veggie Wraps

1 cup prepared hummus
1 cup grated carrots
1 thinly sliced granny smith apple
1 cup packed fresh spinach
2 burrito sized flour tortillas or sandwich wraps

At home lay the tortillas on the counter and spread the hummus on the tortillas. Layer on the other items, fold in tops and bottoms of wraps by about 1 inch, and then roll tightly from one of the open sides to enclose filling. Wrap tightly in plastic or waxed paper. Store in refrigerator and carry in a cooler to the trailhead. Eat for lunch on the first day of your trip.

Serves 1 to 2

Peanut Butter, Chocolate and Banana "Sushi" Wraps

1 large banana
1 packet or 2 Tbsp peanut butter
2 Tbsp mini semi sweet chocolate chips
1 large flour tortilla

Spread the peanut butter on the tortilla. Slice the banana and lay on top. Sprinkle the chips over. Roll up sushi style and cut into pieces with your camp knife.

Serves 1

Peanut Spread

1/2 cup chunky style peanut butter
1/4 cup dry milk
1/4 cup molasses
1 Tbsp honey
1/4 tsp ground cinnamon

Mix well and store in a plastic tub. Eat by the spoonful or serve on your favorite cracker, tortilla or bread.

Couscous Salad with Spinach and Pistachios

In a quart freezer or sandwich bag:
1/2 cup couscous
1/4 cup shelled and diced pistachios
1 Tbsp diced dried shallots or onions
1 tsp dried basil
1/4 tsp ground black pepper
Pinch salt

In a leak proof bottle:
2 Tbsp white wine vinegar
1 Tbsp olive oil

Packed in a sandwich bag:
2 cups fresh baby spinach

FBC method: Add 3/4 cup near boiling water to the dry ingredients. Stir well, seal tightly and let sit for 10 minutes. Fluff up and toss with the dressing and the spinach.

Insulated mug method: Add 3/4 cup boiling water to the dry ingredients and stir well and let sit for 10 minutes. Fluff up and toss with the dressing and spinach.

One pot method: Bring 3/4 cup water to a boil in your pot. Turn off the stove and add in the dry ingredients. Stir well and cover, letting sit for 10 minutes. Fluff up and toss with the dressing and spinach.

Serves 2

Chicken and Bulgur Salad

In a quart freezer or sandwich bag:
1/2 cup bulgur wheat
2 Tbsp diced dried bell pepper
1 Tbsp diced dried onion
1/4 cup dried or freeze-dried pineapple

Also take:
7 ounce pouch chicken breast
1 Tbsp or 1 packet olive oil
2 Tbsp lime juice (1 lime) or 1/2 tsp True Lime© (2 packets) + 2 Tbsp water
Salt and pepper, if desired

FBC method: Add the chicken, lime juice, oil and 3/4 cup near boiling water. Stir well, seal tightly and put in a cozy for 15 minutes. Fluff up and season to taste.

Insulated mug method: Add the chicken, lime juice, oil and 3/4 cup boiling water to the dry ingredients. Stir well, cover tightly and let sit for 15 minutes. Fluff up and season to taste.

One pot method: Bring the chicken, lime juice, oil and 3/4 cup water to a boil in your pot. Turn off the stove and add the dry ingredients. Stir well and cover tightly, let sit for 15 minutes. Fluff up and season to taste.

Serves 1 to 2

Bulgur Almond Cranberry Salad

In a quart freezer bag:
1/2 cup bulgur
1/3 cup sliced almonds
1/4 cup dried sweetened cranberries
1 Tbsp diced dried onion
2 tsp low sodium vegetable bouillon
1/4 tsp ground black pepper

Also take:
1 Tbsp or 1 packet olive oil

FBC method: Add the oil and 3/4 cup near boiling water. Stir well, seal tightly and put in a cozy for 20 minutes. Fluff up.

Insulated mug method: Add the oil and 3/4 cup boiling water to the dry ingredients. Stir well and cover tightly, let sit for 15 to 20 minutes. Fluff up.

One pot method: Bring the oil and 3/4 cup water to a boil in your pot. Turn off the stove and add in the dry ingredients. Stir well, cover tightly and let sit for 15 to 20 minutes. Fluff up.

Serves 1 to 2

Sour Cream Olive Tapenade

In a pint freezer or sandwich bag:
1/4 cup freeze-dried sliced olives
2 Tbsp diced sun-dried tomatoes
1/2 tsp dried parsley

In a small bag:
2 Tbsp sour cream powder

Also take:
1 Tbsp or 1 packet olive oil
Crackers of your choice

Add the oil and 1/2 cup cool water to the bag. Seal tightly and let sit for at least 15 minutes, 30 minutes is preferable. Stir in the sour cream powder till blended. Serve on crackers.

Serves 1 to 2

Creamy Spiced Hummus

Pack in a quart bag:
3/4 cup instant hummus mix
3 Tbsp yogurt powder
1/4 tsp granulated garlic
1/4 tsp paprika powder
1 tsp dried chives

Also take 1 Tbsp or 1 packet olive oil

Add 3/4 cup water and the oil to the hummus mix, stir in well. Add up to 1/4 cup more water to achieve how spreadable of hummus you want.
Serve on wraps or on crackers.

Serves 2

Lemony Chickpea Salad

In a sandwich bag:
1/3 cup cooked and dehydrated chickpeas (garbanzo beans)
2 Tbsp diced sun-dried tomatoes
1 tsp diced dried onion
1/2 tsp parsley
1/4 tsp dried lemon zest
1/4 tsp pr 1 packet True Lemon© powder
1/4 tsp salt
Pinch of ground black pepper

Also take 1 Tbsp or 1 packet olive oil

Add 1/2 cup cool water and the oil to the bag. Seal tightly and let sit for at least an hour to rehydrate. Eat as a salad or use as a filling for a wrap.

Serves 1

Soups

Bacon Potato Chowder

In a sandwich bag:
1/2 cup freeze-dried sweet corn
1/3 cup diced sun-dried tomatoes
2 Tbsp dried onion
2 Tbsp dried celery
1 Tbsp diced dried bell pepper
1 1/2 tsp dried parsley
1/2 tsp granulated sugar
1/4 tsp paprika
1/4 tsp kosher salt
1/4 tsp ground black pepper

In a sandwich bag:
1/2 cup instant mashed potatoes
1/4 cup dry milk
1/4 cup shelf stable bacon

In a pot, combine 3 cups of water and the first bag and bring to a boil. Add in the second bag, stir well, then turn off the stove and let sit tightly covered for 5 minutes.

Serves 2

Tomato Black Bean Soup

Pack in a snack bag:
2 Tbsp tomato powder
2 Tbsp instant black beans
2 tsp potato starch
1/4 tsp kosher salt
1/4 tsp granulated garlic
1/4 tsp chili powder

Insulated mug method: Add 2 cups boiling water to the dry ingredients in a large insulated mug, stirring well. Cover tightly and let sit for 5 minutes.

One pot method: Bring 2 cups water to a boil, turn off the stove and add in the dry ingredients. Stir well, cover tightly and let sit for a couple minutes.

Serves 1 as a meal, 2 as a starter

Veggies and Noodles Soup

Mix well in a large bowl:
3 ounce package finely broken baked ramen or chuka soba noodles
1/2 cup freeze-dried vegetable mix
1/4 cup cooked and dehydrated beans (Navy beans work well)
1 tsp oregano
1 tsp thyme
1 tsp basil
6 tsp lower sodium bouillon of choice
1/4 tsp ground black pepper

Also take:
1 Tbsp or 1 packet olive oil per bag
Shelf stable parmesan cheese to taste
Salt to taste, if desired

Divide the dry ingredients between two sandwich bags evenly (about 1 cup dry mix per bag).

Insulated mug method: Add 1 bag dry ingredients, 1 cup boiling water and 1 Tbsp oil to the mug, stir well, cover tightly and let sit for 5 minutes. Salt to taste and add a sprinkling of cheese on top.

One pot method: Bring to a boil, 2 cups of water plus the oil. Turn off the stove and add in the dry ingredients, stirring well. Cover tightly and let sit for 5 minutes. Salt to taste, if desired and sprinkle cheese on top to taste.

Makes 2 bags, each serves 1 as a meal or 2 as a starter

Beef Curry Noodle Bowl

Pack in a sandwich bag:
3 ounce package baked ramen or chuka soba noodles, crumbled
1/2 cup diced jerky
1/2 cup freeze-dried vegetable mix
1/4 cup raisins (or dried berry mix)
1 Tbsp mild curry powder
2 tsp lower sodium beef bouillon
1/4 tsp granulated garlic

Put 2 cups water in your pot, stir in all the ingredients, then bring to a boil. Let simmer for a couple minutes, turn off the stove, cover tightly and let sit for 5 minutes.

Serves 1 to 2, depending on appetite

Blustery Day Double Potato Chowder

Pack in a sandwich bag:
1 cup dried instant hash browns
1/4 cup diced dried onions
4 tsp low sodium vegetable or beef bouillon
1 tsp dried parsley
1/4 tsp diced dried garlic
1/4 tsp dried thyme
1/4 tsp ground black pepper

Also take:
1 Tbsp or 1 packet olive oil

In a sandwich bag:
1/2 cup instant mashed potato flakes
1/4 cup shelf stable Parmesan cheese
1/2 cup fried onions

Add the vegetable/seasoning bag and 4 cups water to your pot. Cover and set aside for 15 minutes for the vegetables to rehydrate. Add in the oil, stir well and bring to a boil. Set the flame to low, cover and let simmer on a low boil for 5 minutes.

Turn off the stove and add in the cheese/potato bag. Stir in well, taste for seasoning and add more pepper and salt as desired.

Serves 2

Note: Want to make the chowder heartier? Consider adding in a couple servings of shelf stable precooked bacon, found in the salad dressing aisle.

Creamy Tomato Soup

Process in a mini food chopper or blender till combined:
1/2 cup diced sun-dried tomatoes
2 Tbsp dry milk
1 Tbsp tomato powder
1 Tbsp diced dried onions
1 tsp butter powder
1/2 tsp sugar
1/2 tsp Italian seasoning blend
1/4 tsp diced dried garlic
1/4 tsp ground black pepper

Pack in a pint freezer or sandwich bag, adding in 1 Tablespoon bacon bits before sealing the bag.

FBC method: Add 1 cup near boiling water to the freezer bag. Stir well, seal tightly and put in a cozy for 10 minutes.

Insulated mug method: Add 1 cup boiling water to the dry ingredients. Stir well, cover tightly and let sit for 10 minutes.

One pot method: Add dry ingredients to 1-cup water in your pot. Bring to a boil, stirring often. Turn off the heat, cover tightly and let sit for 5 minutes.

For all methods add salt to taste, if desired.

Serves 1

Hearty Minestrone Soup

In a sandwich bag:
1/2 cup precooked and dried small pasta
1/2 cup dehydrated cooked white beans
1/4 cup tomato powder
2 Tbsp shelf stable Parmesan cheese
1 Tbsp diced dried bell peppers
1 tsp diced dried onions
1 tsp diced dried celery flakes
1/4 tsp granulated garlic
1/2 tsp basil
1/2 tsp oregano

Also take:
1 Tbsp or 1 packet olive oil

Add 4 cups water and the oil to dry ingredients in your pot and bring to a boil. Let simmer on low for 5 minutes. Turn off the stove, cover tightly and let sit for 5 minutes.

Serves 2, recipe can be cut in half to make 1 serving

Curried Chicken and Apple Soup

In a sandwich bag:
1/2 cup instant rice
1/4 cup diced dried apples
2 Tbsp diced dried onion
2 Tbsp dried celery flakes
1 Tbsp mild curry powder
1 bay leaf

Also take:
7 ounce pouch chicken
2 Tbsp dry milk
2 Tbsp or 2 packets olive oil

Add the oil, dry ingredients (except for dry milk), chicken and 3 cups water to your pot. Bring to a boil and let simmer gently for 5 minutes. Stir in the dry milk and heat through. Season to taste with salt and pepper if desired.

Serves 2

Note: Celery flakes can be found in the spice aisle. You can also use freeze-dried diced celery instead.

Potato and Cheese Chowder

In a sandwich bag:
1/2 cup dried instant hash browns
1/4 cup diced dried vegetable mix
1/2 cup dry milk
2 Tbsp oat flour (powder oats in a blender)
2 Tbsp flour
1 Tbsp diced dried onion
1 Tbsp wheat germ
1 tsp dried parsley
1/4 tsp salt, if desired
Pinch of black pepper
1/4 cup shelf stable Parmesan cheese

Also take:
1 Tbsp or 1 packet olive oil

Add the dry ingredients, 4 cups of water and the oil into your pot.
Bring to a boil, stirring periodically. Simmer on low for 5 minutes.
Turn off the stove, cover tightly and let sit for 5 minutes.

Serves 2, recipe can be cut in half to serve 1

Beef n' Veggie Stew

In a sandwich bag:
1/4 cup freeze-dried beef, cooked and dehydrated ground beef or 'beef'
TVP
1 1.4-ounce package vegetable soup mix
1/2 cup diced dried mixed vegetables
2 Tbsp couscous
1/2 tsp dried diced garlic

Add 4 cups water and the dry ingredients to your pot. Bring to a boil,
then lower the flame and simmer till vegetables are done.

Serves 2, recipe can be cut in half to serve 1

Note: For the soup mix, brands such as Knorr© work well, if you can
take the salt. Look in the soup aisle or with the gravy packets.

Egg Drop Soup

In a snack size bag:
2 tsp lower sodium vegetable, chicken or beef bouillon
1 Tbsp dried green onion
1 tsp cornstarch
1/4 tsp ground pepper
1/4 tsp dried ginger

In a snack size bag:
1/4 cup commercial dried eggs

1 packet soy sauce

Add 1/2 cup cool water to the egg bag, seal tightly and shake till dissolved. Let sit for 5 to 10 minutes to rehydrate.

Add 2 cups water, the soy sauce packet and the bouillon bag contents to your pot, bring to a boil. Lower the flame to medium low and add in the eggs slowly while stirring gently at the same time. Take off the heat and serve.

Serves 2

Note: Unlike with fresh eggs you won't get the ribbons associated with 'egg drop soup'. If you are hiking in cooler weather or for short trips consider packing in 2 fresh eggs.

Creamy Corn Chowder

In a sandwich bag:
1/2 cup freeze-dried corn
1/2 cup dried potato slices or hash browns
2 Tbsp flour
2 Tbsp dry milk
1 Tbsp diced dried bell peppers
1 tsp dried parsley
1 tsp dried celery flakes
1/2 tsp granulated garlic
1/8 tsp salt, if desired
1/8 tsp paprika
Pinch of black pepper

Also take:
1 tbsp or 1 packet olive oil
2 Tbsp or 4 packets shelf stable Parmesan cheese

Add dry ingredients, 4 cups water and the oil to your pot. Bring to a boil, stirring with a whisk. Let simmer for 5 minutes on low heat. Turn off the heat, cover tightly and let sit for 5 minutes. Top with Parmesan cheese.

Serves 2, recipe can be cut in half to serve 1

American Pho

In a sandwich bag:
3 ounce block ramen (toss seasoning packet) or chuka soba noodles
2 Tbsp crumbled dried mushrooms
2 Tbsp freeze-dried vegetable mix
1 tsp diced dried onion
2 tsp low sodium beef bullion
1 tsp dried parsley
1/4 tsp oregano
1/4 tsp salt, if desired
1/4 tsp granulated garlic
Pinch red pepper flakes
Ground pepper to taste

Also take:
1 to 2 packets (2 to 4 tsp) soy sauce

Add 2 cups water, soy sauce and the dry ingredients to your pot. Bring to a boil. Turn off the heat. Cover tightly and let sit for 5 minutes.

Serves 1 as a meal, 2 as a side cup of soup

Clam Chowder

In a sandwich bag:
1/2 cup dried diced potato
4 tsp low sodium vegetable bouillon
1 tsp dill weed
1/4 tsp granulated garlic
1/4 tsp ground black pepper

In a second bag:
1/4 cup dry milk
2 Tbsp all-purpose flour

Also take:
1 small can clams
1 Tbsp or 1 packet olive oil
2 Tbsp shelf stable parmesan cheese with 1 tsp dried chives mixed in

Add 3 cups water, oil and first bag of ingredients into your pot. Bring to a boil, and then simmer for 5 minutes over low heat.
Meanwhile add 1-cup water to the milk bag and shake up. Stir the milk into the soup, adding in the clams (with any broth).
Heat thru but do not boil, till thickened. Stir in the cheese and salt to taste if desired.

Serves 2

Note: Oysters (smoked or not) can be added instead. Find tins in most canned fish aisles.

Creamy Mushroom Soup

In a sandwich bag:
1/3 cup crumbled dried mushrooms
1/3 cup milk powder
1/4 cup instant rice
2 Tbsp all-purpose flour
2 Tbsp shelf stable Parmesan cheese
1 Tbsp diced dried onion
1 Tbsp dried celery flakes
1 Tbsp dried parsley
4 tsp low sodium vegetable bouillon
1/4 tsp granulated garlic
Dash nutmeg
Dash ground black pepper

Also take:
1 Tbsp or 1 packet olive oil

Add 4 cups water, oil and the dry ingredients to your pot. Bring to a boil, lower heat to low and simmer for 5 minutes, stirring occasionally. Turn the heat off, cover tightly and let sit for 5 minutes. Salt to taste.

Serves 2

Hearty Veggie Stew

In a sandwich bag:
3/4 cup whole wheat couscous
3/4 cup freeze-dried vegetable blend
1/4 cup cooked and dehydrated black eyed peas
3 tsp lower sodium vegetable bouillon

Also take:
2 Tbsp or 2 packets olive oil

Add the dry ingredients, oil and 3 1/2 cups water to your pot. Bring to a boil and let simmer gently for 5 minutes, or until the vegetables and beans are tender. Season to taste with salt and pepper, if desired.

Serves 2

Note: Canned black-eyed peas can be drained, rinsed and dehydrated quickly. Frozen black-eyed peas are sold in many grocery stores and are usually have no salt added for a lower sodium option, dehydrate same as canned.

Seafood Chowder

In a sandwich bag:
1/2 cup dried potatoes (sliced, cubed or hash browns)
1/4 cup diced sun-dried tomatoes
1/4 cup diced dried blend of celery, peppers and carrots
1 Tbsp diced dried onion
4 tsp low sodium vegetable bouillon
1/2 tsp granulated garlic

Also take:
1 can seafood of choice (clams, shrimp, crab)
1 Tbsp or 1 packet olive oil

In a small bag put:
1/4 cup dry milk
1 tsp dried chives

Add 4 cups water and dry vegetables to your pot. Bring to a boil. Cook over low heat, simmering for 5 minutes. Add in pouch of seafood, oil and dry milk. Cook till heated, but not boiling. Remove from heat and let sit tightly covered for 5 minutes. Add salt and pepper to taste, if desired.

Serves 2

Chicken Stew and Dumplings

In a sandwich bag:
1 cup biscuit mix
1 Tbsp dry milk
1 tsp dried chives
1 tsp dried parsley

Mark on bag "Add 1/3 cup water" with a permanent maker.

In a sandwich bag:
1/4 cup diced dried vegetable mix
1 Tbsp diced dried onion flakes
1 Tbsp diced cubed dried potatoes

In a small bag:
4 tsp low sodium chicken bouillon
1/2 tsp dried parsley
1/4 tsp dried thyme
1/4 tsp diced dried garlic
1/4 tsp ground black pepper
Salt to taste

Also take:
7 ounce pouch of chicken.

Cover the vegetables with cold water and let soak for 10-15 minutes. Add 4 cups water, both the broth and vegetable bags and the chicken with any broth to your pan. Bring to a boil, lower the heat a bit on your stove and keep simmering at a low boil. Taste the broth and salt to taste.
Meanwhile, mix up the biscuit mix in its bag. Add the water, push out any air, seal the bag and knead till mixed. Snip a corner on the bag and start squeezing out dumplings. Let them simmer on the soup, with lid on for 5 minutes or till the dumplings are steamed and done.

Serves 2 to 3

Find our biscuit recipes in the breakfast section.

Cheddar Chowder

In a sandwich bag:
1/2 cup dried hash browns
1/3 cup diced dried onion

2 Tbsp all-purpose flour
1 Tbsp dried parsley
1/4 tsp sage
1/4 tsp cumin
1/4 tsp nutmeg
1 bay leaf

Also take:
2 Tbsp or 2 packets olive oil
4 ounces diced cheddar cheese

Add 2 cups of water, oil and dry vegetables to your pot. Bring to a boil and simmer 5 minutes or until vegetables are ready. Add flour mixture slowly, stirring well. Add in the cheese. Simmer and stir over low heat until soup thickens. Do not let it boil.

Serves 2

Hot and Sour Crab Soup

In a sandwich bag:
4 ounces buckwheat soba noodles, broken up
1/4 cup crumbled dried mushrooms
1 Tbsp dried chives
3 tsp low sodium vegetable bouillon
2 tsp diced dried garlic
2 tsp red pepper flakes

Also take:
1/2 cup unseasoned rice vinegar in a leak proof bottle
1 can crabmeat
2 to 3 packets soy sauce (4 to 6 tsp)

Bring 4 cups water and vinegar to a boil in your pot. Add soba noodles
and vegetables to the pot and cook for time on noodle package.
Stir in crabmeat and soy sauce and heat through, but don't boil.

Serves 2 to 3

Chicken and Apple Rice Stew

In a sandwich bag:
1 cup instant brown rice
1/3 cup diced dried apple
1/4 cup diced sun-dried tomato
1 Tbsp diced dried onion
4 tsp low sodium chicken bouillon
2 tsp mild curry powder
1 tsp diced dried garlic
1 tsp dried cilantro
1 tsp dried parsley

Also take:
7-ounce foil pouch chicken

Bring 4 cups water, chicken and the dry ingredients to a boil in your pot. Cook for 5 minutes, stirring occasionally over low heat. Remove from heat, seal tightly and let sit for 5 minutes. Stir well and salt to taste, if desired.

Serves 2 to 3

Chicken Corn Chowder

In a sandwich bag:
1/4 cup diced sun-dried tomatoes
2 Tbsp freeze-dried corn
2 Tbsp diced dried bell peppers
1 Tbsp diced dried onion
1 Tbsp diced dried zucchini
1 tsp diced dried jalapeños
1/4 teaspoon dried thyme
1/4 teaspoon dried dill
1/2 teaspoon dried basil
1/4 tsp diced dried garlic

In a small bag:
1 cup dry milk

Also take:
7-ounce foil pouch of chicken
2 Tbsp or 2 packets olive oil
2 ounces cheddar cheese

Add 4 cups water, oil and vegetables to your pot, let sit for 15 minutes. Bring to a boil, simmer for 5 minutes over low heat, or until vegetables are tender. Add powdered milk and stir well. Heat through until hot, but not boiling. Turn off the heat.
Dice in the cheese and let melt, stirring in.

Serves 2

Beef and Veggie Couscous Soup

In a snack bag:
1/2 cup whole wheat couscous

In a sandwich bag:
2 Tbsp diced sun-dried tomato
1 Tbsp diced dried shallots or onion
1 Tbsp diced dried spinach
1 Tbsp "beef" TVP, freeze-dried hamburger or cooked and dehydrated hamburger
1/4 tsp diced dried garlic
Pinch of thyme

Also take:
2 packets lower sodium beef concentrate or 2 tsp low sodium beef bouillon
Parmesan cheese to taste

Cover the veggies with just enough cool water to cover and let sit for 5 minutes.
Add 2 cups water to your pot and start heating up. Add in the veggie bag along with any remaining water. Bring to a boil, add in the couscous, stirring well. Simmer for a minute over a low flame. Turn off stove and let sit for 5 minutes.
Serve with Parmesan cheese if desired.

Serves 2 small appetites to 1 large appetite

Lentil Stew

In a sandwich bag:
1 cup precooked and dehydrated lentils
2 Tbsp diced dried carrot
2 Tbsp diced dried onion
2 Tbsp diced sun-dried tomatoes
2 Tbsp diced freeze-dried potatoes or instant hash-browns
2 Tbsp tomato powder
1/4 tsp powdered cumin
1/4 tsp diced dried garlic
1/4 tsp ground black pepper
1/4 tsp kosher salt

Add the dry ingredients and 3 cups water to your pot, then bring to a boil. Take off the stove, cover tightly and let sit for 15 minutes.

Serves 2

Clam Florentine Soup

In a sandwich bag:
1/2 cup diced dried spinach
1 cup instant rice
1 Tbsp diced dried onion
1 tsp dried parsley
1 tsp dried basil
1/2 tsp ground black pepper
1/4 tsp or 1 packet True Lime© powder or 1 packet lemon juice

In a snack bag:
1/2 cup shelf stable parmesan cheese
1/3 cup dry milk

Also take:
1 Tbsp or 1 packet olive oil
1 can minced clams

Add 3 1/2 cups water, the oil and sandwich bag ingredients to your pot and bring to a boil. Lower the heat to a low simmer and add in the clams with juice. Heat through until simmering. Stir in the cheese and milk bag until smooth. Season to taste with salt and pepper if desired.

Serves 2

Huckleberry Beef Stew with Dumplings

In a sandwich bag:
6 ounces diced jerky
1/4 cup diced sun-dried tomatoes
2 Tbsp diced dried onions
2 Tbsp diced dried bell peppers
2 Tbsp diced dried carrots
2 Tbsp diced dried celery
1/4 tsp Basil
1/4 tsp Thyme
1/4 tsp Parsley

In a snack bag:
2 Tbsp cornstarch

In a sandwich bag:
1 cup flour
1 tsp baking powder
1 Tbsp vegetable shortening or coconut oil
1/4 tsp salt

In camp pick:
1 cup fresh huckleberries

At home:
Blend the dumpling mix in a small bowl, working the shortening in.

In camp:
Bring 3 cups water and all dry ingredients to a boil in a 2 Liter pot. Simmer for 15 minutes, stir in the berries and bring back to a boil. Mix the cornstarch with a little cold water, stir into the pot to thicken. Add 1/2 cup cool water to the dumpling bag and knead gently to mix. Add on top of the bubbling stew, cover and simmer gently for 10 minutes.

Serves 2

Chicken Lentil Curry

In a sandwich bag:
1 cup cooked and dehydrated lentils
1/2 cup dried instant hash browns
1 Tbsp diced sun-dried tomatoes
1 Tbsp dried green onion
1 Tbsp mild curry powder
1/2 tsp diced dried garlic
1/4 tsp red pepper flakes
1/4 tsp salt

Also take:
5 ounce can chicken
1 Tbsp or 1 packet olive oil

Add 3 cups water, chicken with broth, the oil and lentil bag to your pot
and bring to a boil. Let sit tightly covered for 10 minutes.

Serves 2

Quick Fish Chowder

In a sandwich bag:
3/4 cup instant mashed potatoes
1/2 cup freeze-dried corn
2 Tbsp diced dried red bell pepper
2 Tbsp butter powder
1 Tbsp dried chives
4 tsp lower sodium vegetable or beef bouillon
1/2 tsp ground black pepper

Also take:
3-ounce pouch Albacore tuna
1/4 cup shelf stable Parmesan cheese

Bring 4 cups water to a boil, add in the dry ingredients and stir well, lowering the heat to a gentle simmer. Stir in the tuna and let heat through.
Stir in the cheese and add salt to taste, if desired.

Serves 2

African Peanut Stew

In a sandwich bag:
1/4 cup instant rice
1/4 cup diced dried carrot
2 Tbsp dry onion
3 tsp lower sodium chicken bouillon
1/8 tsp cayenne pepper

Also take:
1/2 cup peanut butter (chunky or smooth)
5-ounce can or 7 ounce pouch chicken

Add 3 cups water, chicken and the dry ingredients to your pot. Bring to a boil, take off the stove and cover tightly. Let sit for 5 minutes, in cool temperatures use a pot cozy. Stir the peanut butter in till smooth.

Serves 2

Lentil and Dumpling Stew

In a sandwich bag:
3/4 cup baking mix
1 Tbsp dry milk
1/4 tsp granulated garlic

In a sandwich bag:
1 cup cooked and dehydrated lentils
2 Tbsp diced dried carrots
2 Tbsp diced freeze-dried potatoes or instant hash browns
1 packet brown or mushroom gravy mix, preferably organic
1/2 tsp ground sage

Add 1/4 cup cool water to the biscuit bag, seal and knead gently till mixed. Bring 2 cups water and the lentil bag and bring to a boil. Lower the flame to low and squeeze or drop the biscuit dough on top (cut the corner off the bag for ease of squeezing). Spread the thick dough out with your spoon. Cover and let simmer gently until the dumplings are cooked through, about 5 minutes. Keep an eye on the lentils, stirring gently under the dumplings to prevent scorching.

Serves 2

High Protein Broth

In a snack size bag:
1 packet Knox© plain gelatin
1 tsp onion powder
1 tsp lower sodium beef bouillon
1/4 tsp granulated garlic
1/8 tsp ground black pepper
Salt to taste

Add dry mix to 1 cup boiling water in your mug. Stir well and let sit till cool enough to sip.

Serves 1, can be easily doubled

Notes: the plain gelatin provides 8 grams of protein per packet and thickens the broth a bit as well. You can use this broth as a base for adding whatever you like or leave it as is. If you have an evening where you are tired and dehydrated a simple cup of broth can help rehydrate you quickly. If you don't watch your sodium intake you can use regular bouillon.

Dinners

Rice Dishes

Warm Chicken Curry Rice Salad

In a sandwich bag:
2 cups instant rice
1/2 cup toasted sunflower seeds
1/4 cup diced dried apple
2 Tbsp diced dried celery or celery flakes
1 Tbsp diced dried carrot

Also take a 7-ounce pouch of chicken

Dressing:
Mix together in a leak proof container -
1/4 cup olive oil
1 tsp brown sugar
1/2 tsp granulated garlic
1 tsp curry powder
1/2 tsp cumin
Pinch of salt

Bring 2 1/4 cups water and the chicken to a boil in your pot. Stir in the dry ingredients; turn off the heat and let sit tightly covered for 15 minutes. Shake the dressing well and toss with the rice.

Serves 2

Chicken Gravy Over Rice

In a quart freezer bag:
2 cups instant rice
1/4 cup freeze-dried peas

In a small bag:
2 Tbsp diced dried onion

In a small bag:
1 Tbsp all-purpose flour
1 tsp low sodium chicken bouillon
1 Tbsp dry milk
Ground black pepper to taste

Also bring:
2 Tbsp or 4 packets shelf stable Parmesan cheese.
1 Tbsp oil
7-ounce pouch chicken

Barely cover the dry onion with cool water in its bag, let sit for 10 minutes.

Add 2 1/4 cups near boiling water to the rice bag. Stir well, seal tightly and put in a cozy for 15 minutes. Heat the oil in your pot over low heat. Sauté the onion till golden, then add the chicken. Mix in the flour bag, and cook for a minute to blend. Add 3/4 cup water slowly, stirring and cook till thick (couple minutes), stirring constantly. Serve over the rice and sprinkle cheese on top.

Serves 2

Notes: You may need to adjust the water and add a little more as needed, if too thick.

Beef And Rice Curry Pilaf

In a sandwich bag:
2 cups instant rice
1/2 cup cooked and dehydrated hamburger or 'Beef' TVP
1/4 cup freeze-dried green beans
1/2 cup diced roasted unsalted cashews
2 Tbsp mild curry powder
1/2 cup dry milk

Also take:
2 ounces diced cheddar cheese

Add 2 3/4 cups water to your pot and bring to a boil. Add in the dry ingredients, stirring well. Turn off the heat, stir in the cheese, cover tightly and put in a pot cozy for 15 minutes. Fluff up before serving.

Serves 2

Greek Spinach Rice

In a sandwich bag:
2 cups instant rice
2 Tbsp tomato powder
2 tsp dried crumbled mint
2 tsp dried crumbled oregano
1 tsp dried thyme
1/4 tsp ground black pepper

In a small bag:
2 Tbsp dry onion

Also take:
6 ounces fresh baby spinach (1 bag)
4 ounces feta cheese, crumbled
2 Tbsp or 2 packets olive oil

Barely cover the onion in its bag with cool water and let sit for 15 minutes to rehydrate.

Heat the oil in your pot over low heat. Sauté onion till tit turns golden. Add 1/4 cup water. Stir in spinach and simmer, covered, for 2 to 3 minutes, until wilted. Stir in 1 3/4 cups water, bring to boil and add the rice bag contents. Stir well and tightly cover. Turn off the stove and put in a pot cozy for 15 minutes. Fluff up and sprinkle the feta cheese over the rice and let sit covered for a couple more minutes to melt.

Serves 2

Notes: This is a first day out meal, due to the produce and cheese in it. This is a great way to impress partners and to try something new. For the spinach grab a 6-ounce bag in the produce department on the way to the trailhead.

Creamy Mushroom Sauce Over Rice

In a quart freezer bag:
2 cups instant rice

In a sandwich bag:
1/4 cup crumbled dried mushrooms
2 Tbsp all-purpose flour
2 Tbsp dry milk
1 Tbsp dried chives
1 1/4 tsp low sodium bouillon
1 tsp dried parsley
1/4 tsp salt, if desired
1/4 tsp granulated garlic
Ground black pepper to taste

Also take:
1 Tbsp or 1 packet olive oil
2 Tbsp shelf stable Parmesan cheese

Add 2 cups near boiling water to the rice bag. Stir, seal tightly and put in a cozy for 15 minutes. Add 1 1/4 cups water and the oil slowly to the dry ingredients in your pot. Stir well and bring to a boil over medium heat. As soon as the sauce thickens, turn the stove off and tightly cover for 5 minutes. Stir the cheese in and serve over the rice.

Serves 2

Pepper Salmon With Rice

In a quart freezer bag:
2 cups instant rice

In a sandwich bag:
1/4 cup dry milk
2 Tbsp shelf stable Parmesan cheese
1 Tbsp dried parsley
1 Tbsp diced dried bell peppers
1/4 tsp ground black pepper
1/4 tsp salt
Pinch of cayenne pepper

Also take:
2 Tbsp or 2 packets olive oil
3 ounce pouch salmon
2 Tbsp flour

Add 2 cups near boiling water to the rice bag. Stir, seal tightly and put in a cozy for 15 minutes. Heat the oil over low heat and whisk the flour in. Cook for a minute. Slowly add 1-cup water to the dry ingredients, stirring well. Bring to a boil while stirring over medium heat. Turn off the stove and crumble in the salmon. Fluff up the rice and serve the sauce over it.

Serves 2

Note: A 3-ounce tuna pouch or smoked salmon may be used instead.

Corn & Chicken Chowder Over Rice

In a quart freezer bag:
2 cups instant rice

In a small bag:
2 Tbsp diced dried onion
1 Tbsp diced dried celery

Also take:
1 Tbsp or 1 packet olive oil

In a small bag:
2 tablespoons all-purpose flour

In a small bag:
1/2 cup freeze-dried corn
1/2 cup dry milk
2 Tbsp shelf stable Parmesan cheese
Salt and pepper to taste

Barely cover the onion and celery with water and let sit for 15 minutes. Add 2 cups near boiling water to the rice bag. Stir well, seal tightly and put into a cozy for 15 minutes.

Heat the oil in your pot over low heat. Add the onion, and celery. Sauté till golden brown. Mix in the flour and cook for a quick minute. Whisk in 1-cup water and contents of corn bag. Bring to a boil over medium heat, stirring till thick. Fluff the rice and serve the sauce over it.

Serves 2

Fondue Rice

In a quart freezer bag:
2 cups instant rice

In a sandwich bag:
1/2 cup dry milk
2 Tbsp all-purpose flour
1 tsp dried parsley
1 tsp dried chives
1 tsp diced dried onion
1/2 tsp diced dried garlic
1/4 tsp salt
1/4 tsp dry mustard powder
Pinch of cayenne pepper

Also take 3 ounces Swiss cheese.

Add 2 cups near boiling water to the rice bag. Stir, seal tightly and put in a cozy for 10 minutes. Add 1 3/4 cups water and the dry ingredients to your pot, stir well and bring to just bubbling on medium heat. Dice up the cheese and stir in. Turn off the stove and let sit till melted. Fluff up the rice and serve over it.

Serves 2

Orange Chicken Rice

In a sandwich bag:
2 cups instant rice
1/2 cup freeze-dried oranges
2 Tbsp shredded coconut
1 Tbsp diced dried onion
2 tsp low sodium chicken bouillon
1 tsp soy sauce powder
Pinch red pepper flakes

Also take a 3 ounce can chicken

Bring 2 1/2 cups water and chicken with and broth to a boil in your pot. Add in the dry ingredients and turn off the stove. Stir well, tightly cover and put in a pot cozy for 15 minutes. Fluff up before serving.

Serves 2

Notes: If you cannot get soy sauce powder, substitute regular or lower sodium soy sauce. You will want to start with 1 Tbsp and add to taste. Kirk enjoys this recipe with Pad Thai sauce on top. It gives the rice a hint of sweetness with low heat. Pad Thai sauce can be carried for a couple days in a leak proof container. Find it in Asian grocery stores imported from Thailand.

Coastal Shrimp Rice

In a sandwich bag:
2 cups instant rice
2 Tbsp diced dried bell peppers
2 Tbsp diced dried onions
1 Tbsp diced dried celery
1/4 tsp dill weed
1/4 tsp thyme
1/4 tsp granulated garlic
Salt and pepper to taste

Also take:
1 Tbsp olive oil
1 can tiny shrimp, drained
2 Tbsp or 4 packets shelf stable Parmesan cheese

Add 2 1/4 cups water, shrimp and oil to your pot and bring to a boil.
Add in the rice and seasoning bag, stirring well. Turn off the heat,
cover tightly and let sit for 15 minutes in a pot cozy. Fluff up the rice
and top with the cheese.

Serves 2

Broccoli Walnut Chicken Rice

In a sandwich bag:
2 cups instant rice
1/2 tsp granulated garlic
1 tsp dried thyme
1/4 cup diced dried broccoli
1 Tbsp diced dried onion
1/4 cup diced walnuts
2 tsp low sodium chicken bouillon
1 Tbsp dry chicken gravy mix

Also take:
5-ounce can of chicken
1 Tbsp or 1 packet olive oil
2 Tbsp or 4 packets shelf stable Parmesan cheese

Add the oil, the chicken with its broth and 2 cups water to your pot. Bring to a boil and add in the dry ingredients, stirring well. Turn off the stove and let sit tightly covered for 15 minutes in a pot cozy.

Fluff up the rice and top with the cheese.

Serves 2

Pineapple and Chicken Curry

In a snack bag put:
1/2 cup dried pineapple chunks
2 Tbsp diced dried red bell pepper
2 Tbsp diced dried onion
1/4 tsp diced dried jalapeño
1/2 tsp dried garlic

Also take:
1 tsp mild curry powder (in small bag)
1 Tbsp or 1 packet vegetable oil
7-ounce foil pouch chicken
1 mini "airline size" bottle of rum

In a quart freezer bag take:
2 cups instant rice

Cover the dried vegetables and fruit with 1/2 cup cool water and let sit for 15 minutes. Drain off any remaining water. Meanwhile, open the chicken pouch and pour the rum in, let sit. Add 2 cups water near boiling water to the rice, stir, seal tightly and put in a cozy for 15 minutes. In your pot heat the oil over medium heat and cook the vegetables and curry powder for a couple minutes till hot. Lower the flame, add the chicken and heat through. Divide the rice and top with the sauce.

Serves 2

Curry Tuna Rice

In a sandwich bag take:
2 cups instant rice
1/2 cup golden raisins
1 Tbsp coconut cream powder
2 tsp mild curry powder
Pinch salt

Also bring:
3-ounce pouch Albacore tuna
1 hard-boiled egg (Optional, first night out)

Bring 2 1/2 cups water to a boil in your pot. Add in the rice bag and tuna, stir well and cover tightly for 15 minutes. In colder weather use a pot cozy to insulate.
Meanwhile, peel the egg and finely chop. Fluff up the rice and mix the egg in.

Serves 2

Trail Fried Rice

In a quart freezer bag:
2 cups instant rice
1 cup freeze-dried mixed vegetables
2 tsp low sodium chicken bullion
1 Tbsp dried chives
1 tsp granulated garlic
1/4 tsp of ground ginger

Also take:
7-ounce pouch of chicken
2 Tbsp or 2 packets oil
2 eggs, in shell (first night out they are fine)
2 packets soy sauce

Add 2 3/4 cups near boiling water into the freezer bag. Stir well, seal tightly and put in a cozy for 15 minutes. Heat oil in a trail wok or 2 Liter non-stick pot over medium heat, add eggs, cook until done, stirring occasionally. Lower heat if you can to low. If you cannot, keep the pan moving constantly over the heat. Stir in rice, chicken and soy sauce. Toss till mixed. Remove from heat.

Serves 2

Notes: To make long term shelf stable replace the fresh eggs with 2 eggs worth of commercial whole dried eggs. Follow package directions on how much dry powder per egg and how much water. Pack the dry powder in a small bag. When ready to cook, add water called for to the bag, seal tightly and shake to dissolve. Proceed as with fresh eggs.

Hearty Fall Gravy

In a quart freezer bag:
2 cups instant rice
In a sandwich bag:
1/4 cup freeze-dried beef, cooked and dehydrated ground beef or 'beef' TVP
1/4 cup diced sun-dried tomatoes
2 Tbsp diced dried bell peppers
2 Tbsp crumbled dried mushrooms
2 tsp diced dried onion
1/2 tsp sugar

Also take:
1 packet mushroom gravy mix, preferably organic

Cover the vegetables in their bag with 1/2 cup cool water and let sit for 30 minutes. Bring two cups water to a near boil. Add it to the rice bag, seal tightly and put in a cozy for 15 minutes. Add 1-cup water to your pot with the gravy mix, stir well. Add in the vegetable bag contents. Bring to a boil and cook for time on gravy package.
Divide the rice and serve the gravy over it.

Serves 2

Spam Fried Rice

In a quart freezer bag:
1 cup instant rice
1 Tbsp diced dried shallots or onions
2 Tbsp diced dried carrots
2 Tbsp freeze-dried green beans
2 Tbsp freeze-dried corn
1 tsp dried chives
1/2 tsp diced dried garlic
1/4 tsp red pepper flakes
1/4 tsp dried powdered ginger

Also take:
1 to 2 packets or 1 to 2 tsp soy sauce
1 single serving Spam packet
1 Tbsp or 1 packet oil
2 fresh eggs or commercial dried eggs, packed in a small bag.

Bring 1 1/2 cups water to a near boil. Add to the rice bag, stir well, seal tightly and put in a cozy for 15 to 20 minutes. If using dried eggs, follow the directions to rehydrate 2 eggs worth. Add the water, seal tightly and shake to dissolve.

Heat the oil in your pot and add in the Spam. Cube up and stir-fry till turning golden. Add in the cooked rice and stir constantly till smelling great. Splash on the soy sauce and mix in. Make a hole in the center and add in the egg mixture. If using fresh eggs, crack into the hole. Start scrambling them and then toss with the rice. Pull off the heat as soon as the eggs are setting up.

Serves 2

Rice & Tomato Chicken Pilaf

In a quart freezer or sandwich bag:
1 cup instant white rice
2 Tbsp diced sun-dried tomatoes
1 Tbsp tomato powder
1 Tbsp diced dried onion
1/4 teaspoon dried thyme
1/4 tsp ground black pepper

Also take:
7-ounce pouch chicken breast
1 Tbsp or 1 packet olive oil
2 Tbsp or 4 packets shelf stable Parmesan cheese

FBC method: Add the chicken, oil and 1 1/4 cups near boiling water. Stir well, seal tightly and put in a cozy for 15 minutes. Fluff up and sprinkle with the cheese.

Insulated mug method: Add the chicken, oil and 1 1/4 cups boiling water to the dry ingredients. Stir well, cover tightly and let sit for 15 minutes. Fluff up and sprinkle with the cheese.

One pot method: Bring the chicken, oil and 1 1/4 cups water to a boil in your pot. Turn off the stove and add in the dry ingredients. Stir well, cover tightly and let sit for 15 minutes. In cold temperature insulate your pot in a pot cozy. Fluff up and sprinkle with the cheese.

Serves 1 to 2

Indian Red Curry

In a quart freezer bag:
1 1/2 cups instant rice

In a small bag:
2 Tbsp tomato powder
1 tsp ground ginger

Also take:
6-ounce container plain yogurt
7-ounce pouch chicken

In a small bag:
1/4 cup slivered almonds or cashews

In a small bag:
2 Tbsp mild red curry paste

Bring to a boil in your pot 1 1/2 cups water. Let cool for a few seconds and add to the rice bag, stir and seal tightly. Put in a cozy for 15 minutes. Meanwhile combine tomato powder, ginger, curry paste, yogurt and chicken. Bring to a gentle boil in your pot over a medium flame. Serve the sauce over the rice and top with the nuts.

Serves 2

Note: An unopened container of yogurt will be fine for 1 to 2 days on the trail in temperatures below 70°F. For safer carrying fill a freezer bag with ice cubes and stash the unopened yogurt cup in the bag, seal tightly.

Sweet and Sour Chicken over Rice

In a snack bag:
1/4 cup diced dried chewy sweetened pineapple
1 Tbsp diced candied ginger
1 Tbsp diced dried bell peppers
1 Tbsp dried celery flakes
1 tsp cornstarch
1/4 tsp dried garlic

In a quart freezer bag:
1 1/2 cups instant rice (or dehydrated Jasmine rice)

Also take:
7-ounce package chicken

In a leak proof bottle:
3 Tbsp unseasoned rice vinegar
1 Tbsp lower sodium soy sauce
1 Tbsp honey

Bring 1 1/2 cups water to a near boil; add it to the rice bag. Seal tightly
and put in a cozy for 15 minutes. Meanwhile in your pot combine the
dry ingredients with ¾ cup water. Shake up the liquid sauce in the
bottle and add in. Bring to a boil stirring often. Lower the heat to low
and add in the chicken. Heat through. Serve the sauce over the rice.

Serves 2

Two Rice & Lentil Pilaf

In a quart freezer or sandwich bag:
1/2 cup instant white rice
1/2 cup instant brown rice
1/4 cup diced sun-dried tomatoes
2 Tbsp cooked and dried lentils
1/4 tsp diced dried garlic
1/4 tsp ground black pepper
1 1/4 tsp lower sodium vegetable bouillon

Also take 2 packets or 1 Tbsp shelf stable Parmesan cheese

FBC method: Add 1 1/4 cups near boiling water. Stir well, seal tightly and put in a cozy for 15 minutes. Fluff up and top with the cheese.

Insulated mug method: Add 1 1/4 cups boiling water. Stir well, cover tightly and put in a cozy for 15 minutes. Fluff up and top with the cheese.

One pot method: Add 1 1/4 cups water to your pot and bring to a boil. Add in the dry ingredients, stir well, cover tightly and turn off the heat and let sit for 15 minutes. Fluff up and top with the cheese. In cold weather, put the pot in a pot cozy.

Serves 1

Chicken with Brown Rice

In a quart freezer or sandwich bag:
1 1/2 cups instant brown rice
1/2 cup freeze-dried green peas
2 Tbsp shelf stable Parmesan cheese
1 Tbsp butter powder
2 tsp low sodium chicken bouillon
1/2 tsp diced dried garlic
1/4 tsp ground black pepper

Also take:
5-ounce can or 7 ounce pouch chicken breast
1 Tbsp or 1 packet olive oil

FBC method: Bring 2 cups water to a near boil. Add the chicken with broth, oil and water to the bag. Stir well, seal tightly and put in a cozy for 15 minutes.

Insulated mug method: Bring 2 cups water to a boil. In a large mug add the chicken with broth, oil and the water to the dry ingredients. Stir well, cover tightly and let sit for 15 minutes.

One pot method: Bring the chicken with broth, oil and water to a boil in your pot. Take off the heat and add in the dry ingredients. Cover tightly and let sit for 15 minutes. In cool weather use a pot cozy.

Serves 1 to 2

Bacon and Pepper Risotto

In a quart freezer or sandwich bag:
1 cup instant rice
2 Tbsp diced dried bell peppers
1 Tbsp shelf stable bacon bits
1 Tbsp shelf stable Parmesan cheese
1 tsp lower sodium vegetable or beef bouillon
1/4 tsp True Lemon powder

FBC method: Add 1 cup near boiling water to the bag. Stir well, seal tightly and put in a cozy for 15 minutes.

Insulated mug method: Add the ingredients to your mug along with 1 cup boiling water. Stir well, cover tightly and let sit for 15 minutes.

One pot method: Bring 1 cup water to a boil in your pot and turn off your stove. Add in the dry ingredients. Stir well, cover tightly and let sit for 10 minutes. In cool weather or at high altitude use a pot cozy.

Serves 1

Artichoke Infused Rice

In a quart freezer or sandwich bag:
1 cup instant rice
1/4 cup freeze-dried mixed vegetables
2 Tbsp shelf stable Parmesan cheese
1/4 tsp onion powder
1/4 tsp dried diced garlic
1/8 tsp dry marjoram
1/8 tsp salt
1/4 tsp black pepper
1/4 tsp dry thyme

Pack in a small bag:
1/4 cup diced roasted and lightly salted cashews

Pack in a sandwich bag with liquid:
6 ounce jar marinated artichokes

FBC method: Add 1 1/4 cups near boiling water and the artichokes with liquid. Stir well, seal tightly and put in a cozy for 15 minutes. Stir in nuts and toss well.

One pot method: Add the artichokes with liquid to your pot. Bring to a boil, add in rice bag and stir well. Take off the heat, cover tightly and let sit for 15 minutes. Stir in the nuts and toss well. In cool weather use a pot cozy to retain heat.

Serves 1

Note: Marinated artichokes will carry for a day or two, for long term carrying leave in their jar for safety. You will want to double bag to avoid a spill, we recommend carrying in your mug or similar to protect.

Shrimp Sauce over Rice

In a quart freezer bag:
2 cups instant rice

In a sandwich bag:
1/2 cup diced dried celery
1/4 cup crumbled dried mushrooms

In a snack bag:
1 Tbsp cornstarch
2 tsp lower sodium chicken bouillon

Also take
1 can or pouch tiny shrimp, drained
1 packet hot sauce of choice

Cover the vegetables with 3/4 cup cool water in the bag. Seal tightly and let sit for 30 minutes. Bring 2 cups water to a near boil and add to the rice. Seal tightly and put in a cozy for 15 minutes. Add 2 Tbsp cool water to the cornstarch bag, seal tightly and shake to dissolve, set aside. Add 1-cup water to your pot along with the rehydrated vegetables. Bring to a boil, lower the flame and add in the shrimp. Heat through, add in the cornstarch mixture and cook till thickened. Add hot sauce to taste. Divide the rice and serve the sauce over it.

Serves 2

Tropical Spam

In a sandwich bag:
1 cup instant rice
1/4 cup diced sweetened dried pineapple
1/4 cup shredded coconut

Also take:
1 Spam Single packet
1 soy sauce packet

Heat your pot over a medium flame and drop the Spam in. Break it up into bite size pieces while it heats through and gets browned. Add in 1 1/4 cups water and soy sauce; bring to a boil. Add in the dry ingredients, stir well, turn off the stove, cover tightly and let sit for 15 minutes. Fluff up before serving.

Serves 1

Bacon n' Egg Rice

In a sandwich bag:
1/3 cup dried egg powder
1 tsp dried parsley

In a sandwich bag:
1 1/2 cups instant rice
1/4 cup crumbled dried mushrooms
1 Tbsp bacon bits
1 tsp dried celery flakes
2 tsp diced dried onion

Also take 1 to 2 soy sauce packets

Cook rice in 1 1/2 cups water with bacon. Mix the egg with 1/3 cup water, seal tightly and shake to mix. Pour into the cooked rice and stir over low flame till cooked.
Season to taste with soy sauce.

Serves 2

Notes: Find egg powder online, such as Ova brand. You can also take 2 to 3 fresh eggs instead.

Creamy Turkey and Rice

In a sandwich or quart freezer bag:
1 cup instant rice
1/4 cup freeze-dried or dehydrated canned turkey
1 Tbsp diced sun-dried tomatoes
2 tsp turkey gravy powdered mix, preferably organic
1 tsp dried parsley
1/4 tsp granulated garlic

Also take:
1 Tbsp or 1 packet olive oil
2 packets or 1 Tbsp shelf stable Parmesan cheese

FBC method: Add 1 1/4 cups near boiling water and the oil to the freezer bag. Stir well, seal tightly and put in a cozy for 15 minutes. Stir well and sprinkle the cheese on top.

Insulated mug method: In a large insulated mug add the dry ingredients, oil and 1 1/4 cups boiling water. Stir well, cover tightly and let sit for 15 minutes. Stir well and sprinkle the cheese on top.

One pot method: Bring 1 1/4 cups water and oil to a boil and add in the dry ingredients. Stir well, cover tightly and let sit for 15 minutes. In cooler temperatures use a pot cozy. Stir well and sprinkle the cheese on top.

Serves 1

Alfredo Beef Rice

In a sandwich or quart freezer bag:
1 cup instant rice
2 Tbsp freeze-dried roast beef cubes
2 Tbsp freeze-dried or dehydrated crumbled spinach
2 Tbsp Alfredo powder mix
1 Tbsp dry milk
1/4 tsp granulated garlic

Also take:
1 Tbsp or 1 packet olive oil
2 packets or 1 Tbsp shelf stable Parmesan cheese

FBC method: Add 1 1/4 cups near boiling water and the oil to the freezer bag. Stir well, seal tightly and put in a cozy for 15 minutes. Stir well and sprinkle the cheese on top.

Insulated mug method: In a large insulated mug add the dry ingredients, oil and 1 1/4 cups boiling water. Stir well, cover tightly and let sit for 15 minutes. Stir well and sprinkle the cheese on top.

One pot method: Bring 1 1/4 cups water and oil to a boil and add in the dry ingredients. Stir well, cover tightly and let sit for 15 minutes. In cooler temperatures use a pot cozy. Stir well and sprinkle the cheese on top.

Serves 1

Saffron Chicken Rice

In a quart freezer bag:
1 cup cooked and dehydrated Jasmine rice
1 Tbsp diced dried onion
1 tsp low sodium vegetable or chicken bouillon
1/2 tsp ground cardamom
1/8 tsp ground saffron
pinch of cayenne pepper

Also take:
1 Tbsp or 1 packet extra virgin olive oil
3 ounce can chicken

FBC method: Add 1 cup near boiling water and the chicken to the freezer bag. Stir well, seal tightly and put in a cozy for 15 minutes.

Insulated mug method: In a large insulated mug add the dry ingredients, the chicken and 1 cup boiling water. Stir well, cover tightly and let sit for 15 minutes

One pot method: Bring 1-cup water and the chicken to a boil and add in the dry ingredients. Stir well, cover tightly and let sit for 15 minutes. In cooler temperatures use a pot cozy.

Chickpea Marinara Rice

In a quart freezer bag:
1 cup instant rice

In a quart freezer bag:
1/2 cup cooked and dehydrated chickpeas
2 Tbsp diced sun-dried tomatoes
2 Tbsp tomato powder
1 tsp diced dried onion
1 tsp parsley flakes
1 tsp Italian seasoning blend
1 tsp granulated sugar
1/4 tsp granulated garlic
1/4 tsp ground black pepper
1/4 tsp salt

Also take:
1 Tbsp or 1 packet olive oil
2 Parmesan cheese packets

FBC method:
Add 1-cup near boiling water to the rice bag, stirring well. Add the oil to the chickpea bag and 1 cup near boiling water. Seal both bags tightly and put in a cozy for 15 minutes.
Serve the sauce over the rice, sprinkle with the cheese.

Serves 1 large appetite or 2 smaller ones

Polenta Dishes

Bacon & Cheddar Polenta

In a sandwich bag:
3/4 cup yellow cornmeal
2 Tbsp shelf stable crumbled bacon or bacon TVP
1 Tbsp diced dried onion
1/2 tsp diced dried garlic
Black pepper to taste

Also take:
2 ounces cheddar cheese, diced up.

Bring 2 cups water to a boil in the your pot. As soon as the water boils, lower the heat on your stove to low. Add in the dry ingredients. Using a whisk, stir rapidly till the polenta is smooth. Cook over the low flame for 3 minutes. Turn off the stove and stir in the cheese. Put the lid on the pot and let sit for a few minutes. You may need to keep the pot above the flame. Serve topped with a bit more bacon if desired.

Serves 2

Bacon & Cheddar Polenta Instant Style

In a quart freezer or sandwich bag:
2 packets instant grits
1 Tbsp shelf stable crumbled bacon or bacon TVP
1 Tbsp diced dried onion
1/4 tsp diced dried garlic
1/4 tsp ground black pepper

Also take:
1 ounce cheddar cheese

FBC method: Add 1 cup near boiling water. Stir well, seal tightly and put in a cozy for 10 minutes. Dice the cheese and fold in, stirring well.

Insulated mug method: Add 1 cup boiling water to the dry ingredients. Stir well, cover tightly and let sit for 10 minutes. Dice the cheese and fold in, stirring well.

Serves 1

Double Corn Polenta

In a sandwich bag:
1/2 cup cornmeal
1/3 cup dry milk
1/4 cup freeze-dried corn
1/4 tsp ground black pepper

Also take:
2 Tbsp or 4 packets shelf stable Parmesan cheese

Bring 1 1/2 cups water to a boil in your pot. As soon as the water boils, lower the heat on your stove to low. Add in the dry ingredients. Using a whisk, stir rapidly till the polenta is smooth. Cook over the low flame for 3 minutes. Turn off the stove and stir in the cheese. Put the lid on the pot and let sit for a few minutes. You may need to keep the pot above the flame. This makes a thick polenta, you may like up to an additional 1/4 cup water whisked in while cooking for a softer texture. Whisk in the cheese and season to taste if desired.

Serves 1

Double Corn Polenta Instant Style

In a quart freezer or sandwich bag:
2 packets instant grits
1/3 cup dry milk
1/4 cup freeze-dried corn
1/4 tsp ground black pepper

Also take:
2 Tbsp or 4 packets shelf stable Parmesan cheese

FBC method: Add 1 1/4 cups near boiling water and stir well. Seal tightly and put in a cozy for 15 minutes. Stir in the cheese.

Insulated mug method: Add 1 1/4 cups boiling water to the dry ingredients. Stir well, seal tightly and let sit for 15 minutes. Stir in the cheese.

Serves 1

Oat Dishes

Savory Oats

In a sandwich bag:
1/2 cup quick cooking oats
1/4 tsp ground black pepper
Pinch salt

Also take:
2 Tbsp or 4 packets shelf stable Parmesan cheese

Bring 1 cup water to a boil in your pot. Turn the stove down to low and add in the dry ingredients. Stir well for a minute, lifting the stove above the flame if needed. Stir in the cheese. Let sit and cool down for a minute before eating.

Serves 1

Savory Oat Cakes

Follow the above directions to make the oats. Let sit till cold, then divvy up into portions.
Heat up your fry pan or pot and heat some oil up over a medium flame. Add the cold oats into the pot carefully and cook till crispy and browned. Drizzle a bit more oil on top and flip over, repeating till done.

Serves 1

Oat and Nut Pan Patties

In a gallon storage or freezer bag:
1 cup dry breadcrumbs (plain or Italian flavor)
1 cup quick cooking oats
1 cup cashews, almonds, walnuts or pecans, finely ground
1/4 cup all-purpose flour
1 1/2 tsp Italian seasoning blend

Also take:
2 Tbsp or 2 packets cashew, almond, sunflower or peanut butter
2 Tbsp or 2 packets oil

Add the cashew butter to the bag, knead or stir in, then add 1-cup cool water slowly, gently kneading. Let sit for 15 minutes hydrate. If dry, knead in a little more water.
Heat half the oil in your pot over a medium flame, scoop or drop out balls of mix into the pot, flatten into a patty shape with your spoon. Cook till browned, flip over and cook till browned as well. Eat as, dipping in a favorite sauce is or serve as a filling in a tortilla wrap.

Serves 2 to 4

Barley Dishes

Chicken and Barley Curry

In a sandwich bag:
1 cup cooked and dehydrated barley
3/4 cup freeze-dried chicken
3/4 cup diced dried mixed vegetables
1/2 cup diced dried apples
3 tsp lower sodium chicken bouillon
1 Tbsp mild curry powder

In a snack bag:
1/2 cup shredded coconut
1/2 cup raisins
1/2 cup diced roasted cashews

Bring 3 cups water to a boil in your pot and add in the dry ingredient bag. Lower the heat and simmer gently for 5 minutes covered. Put in a pot cozy for another 5 minutes. Fluff up and divide into two servings and top with the coconut, raisins and cashews.

Serves 2

Savory Pancakes

Savory Pizza Pancakes

In a quart freezer bag:
2 cups baking mix
1/3 cup dry milk
1/2 cup freeze-dried mozzarella cheese

In a small bag:
2 Tbsp diced dried bell peppers
2 Tbsp diced sun-dried tomatoes
2 tsp Italian herb seasoning

Also take:
5-ounce pouch pizza sauce (look for shelf stable by Boboli)
1 packet shelf stable pepperoni slices
2 Tbsp or 2 packets vegetable oil

To the dried veggie bag add 1/4 cup cool water. Seal tightly and let sit for at least 15 minutes to rehydrate.
Add the pepperoni slices and the contents of the veggie bag to the freezer bag along with 1 cup water. Knead or stir the bag till well combined.

Coat your fry pan with oil and heat over medium flame. Cut a corner off your bag and squeeze 4-inch circles of batter into pan. Cook 2 minutes or until bubbles form on top. Flip with a spatula and cook 1 minute more or until pancakes are golden brown. Repeat till done. You may need to lower the stove's heat and /or keep the fry pan above the flame to prevent scorching. Serve with pizza sauce on top!

Serves 2.

Notes: Shelf stable pepperoni slices can be found in most grocery stores, often in the refrigerated section next to the bacon. Look for "refrigerate after opening" on the packaging. Hormel makes a 3 1/2 ounce package that contains 2 interior packets. Take one for the recipe.

Potato Dishes

Shepherd's Pie

In a quart freezer bag:
1 1/2 cups instant mashed potatoes
1/2 cup dry milk
1/2 tsp granulated garlic
1/4 tsp salt, if desired

In a small sandwich bag:
1/2 cup cooked and dehydrated hamburger or "beef" TVP
2 Tbsp diced sun-dried tomatoes

In another small bag:
1/4 cup freeze-dried vegetables (mixed or green beans work well)
1 Tbsp dried onion
1 package organic brown gravy mix
1/2 tsp oregano

Also take:
1 Tbsp or 1 packet olive oil
2 ounces diced cheddar cheese

Add 1/2 cup cool water to the ground beef/tomatoes to rehydrate. Any excess water can be used in the dinner. Set aside for 10 minutes.

Add 2 cups near boiling water to the freezer bag. Stir well, seal tightly and put in a cozy to keep warm. Put vegetable bag contents into your pot, hamburger bag contents, oil and 1 1/2 cups water. Stir well and heat to boiling, stirring, and then simmer on low heat 1 minute or so, until the gravy thickens. Fluff the potatoes and place on the filling. Top with the cheese.

Serves 2

Note: You can also scoop the potatoes into two pint freezer bags or bowls, then spoon the gravy onto them.

Masman Curry Over Garlic Mashers

In a small bag:
1 Tbsp Thai-style Masman curry paste

In a small bag:
1/4 cup diced dried carrots
1 Tbsp diced dried onion
1/4 cup cooked & dehydrated garbanzo beans

1.75 ounce pouch coconut cream powder

In a small bag:
1 Tbsp brown sugar
1/3 cup diced peanuts

In a quart freezer bag:
1 1/2 cups instant mashed potatoes
1/2 cup dry milk
1 tsp diced dried garlic
1/4 tsp salt

Add 1/2 cup cool water to the bean and vegetable bag. Let sit and rehydrate for 15 to 30 minutes.

Bring 2 cups water to a near boil, add to the potatoes and stir well. Seal tightly and put in a cozy to keep warm. In your pot add curry paste, coconut powder and 1-cup water and bring to a boil. Add bean and vegetable bag along with sugar and nuts. Cook until sugar is dissolved and the sauce is bubbling. Serve over the mashed potatoes.

Serves 2

Cheesy Leek and Bacon Mashers

In a small bag:
2 Tbsp butter

Also take:
2 leeks

In a sandwich bag:
1/4 cup powered milk
1 cup instant mashed potatoes

Also take:
1/4 cup shelf stable crumbled bacon
2 ounces diced white cheddar cheese
Salt and pepper

Dice the leeks and set aside. Melt the butter in your pot and sauté leeks until tender and translucent over low heat. Add in 1 1/2 cups water and bring to a boil. Remove from heat and stir in potato bag contents, bacon and cheese. Add salt and pepper to taste, if desired.

Serves 2

Notes: For extended trips you can carry Ghee butter, which is shelf stable. For the leeks, carry 2 Tbsp dried chopped leeks in a small bag. Rehydrate by covering with room temperature water for 10 minutes. Drain and proceed as above.

Hamburger Gravy

In a quart freezer bag:
1 1/2 cups instant mashed potatoes
1/2 cup dry milk
Pinch of salt

In a small bag:
1/2 cup "beef TVP" or cooked and dehydrated or freeze-dried hamburger

In a small bag:
3 Tbsp all-purpose flour
2/3 cup dry milk
1 Tbsp dried onions
1/2 tsp granulated garlic
1 tsp dried chives
1/4 tsp salt
Ground black pepper
2 Tbsp shelf stable Parmesan cheese

Also take 1 Tbsp or 1 packet olive oil

Add 1/2 cup cool water to the hamburger bag. Let sit and rehydrate for 10 minutes. Add 2 cups near boiling water to the freezer bag with potatoes. Stir well, seal tightly and put in a cozy to keep warm. Add 2 cups water and oil into your pot. Add the dry mix, stirring with a whisk. Add in the hamburger and keep stirring till it gets thick. Serve the gravy over the potatoes.

Serves 2

Mashed Potato Burritos

In a quart freezer or sandwich bag:
3/4 cup instant mashed potatoes
1 Tbsp dry milk
1 Tbsp butter powder
1 Tbsp sour cream powder

Also take:
2 soft taco sized flour tortillas
Salsa to taste
1 to 2 ounces of cheddar, Co-jack or Pepper Jack cheese

Freezer bag method: Add 1 cup near boiling water to the quart freezer bag. Stir well, seal tightly and let sit in a cozy while you prep the cheese.

Insulated mug method: Add the dry ingredients to your mug along with 1 cup near boiling water. Stir well and let sit while you prep the cheese.

For both methods: Slice the cheese up. Lay down a section of clean paper towel. Place your tortillas down. Spread the mashed potatoes between the two tortillas. Top with cheese, then salsa. Roll up and eat.

Serves 1

Colcannon Mashers

In a sandwich or quart freezer bag:
3/4 cup instant mashed potatoes
2 Tbsp butter powder
2 Tbsp dry milk
2 Tbsp shelf stable bacon or bacon bits
2 Tbsp dried shredded cabbage
1 Tbsp dried diced shallots or onions
1 tsp dried parsley
1/4 tsp ground black pepper
Salt to taste

FBC method: Add 1 1/4 cups near boiling water to the bag. Stir well, getting into the corners. Seal tightly and put in a cozy for 15 minutes. Stir again before serving.

Insulated mug method: Add 1 1/4 cups boiling water to the dry ingredients. Stir well, cover tightly and let sit for 15 minutes. Stir again before serving.

One pot method: Bring 1 1/4 cups water to a boil. Turn off the stove and in the dry ingredients. Stir well, cover tightly and let sit for 15 minutes. Stir again before serving. In cold temperatures you may want to put your pot in a pot cozy.

Salt to taste, if desired.

Serves 1

Cheese Steak Mashers

In a quart freezer or sandwich bag:
2/3 cup instant mashed potatoes
1/4 cup dry milk
2 Tbsp shelf stable Parmesan cheese
1 Tbsp diced dried bell peppers
1 Tbsp diced dried onions
1/8 tsp red pepper flakes

Also take 1 snack size bag jerky (1 1/2 ounces)

FBC method: Cut or tear the jerky into small bits, add to the bag. Bring 1 1/4 cups water to a near boil. Add the water slowly, stirring. Seal tightly and put in a cozy for 15 minutes.

Insulated mug method: Cut or tear the jerky into small bits, adding to your mug with the dry ingredients. Bring 1 1/4 cups water to a boil; add slowly to the dry ingredients, stirring well. Cover tightly and let sit for 15 minutes.

One pot method: Cut or tear the jerky into small bits. Add it and 1 1/4 cups water to your pot and bring to a boil. Take off the heat and stir in the dry ingredients. Cover and let sit for 10 minutes.

Serves 1

Hiker Trash Potatoes

Pack in a quart freezer or sandwich bag:
1/4 cup freeze-dried ground beef
1/2 cup freeze-dried green beans
1 1/2 cups instant mashed potatoes
2 Tbsp dry milk
1 packet brown gravy mix, preferably organic

FBC method: Add 3 cups boiling water, stir well seal tightly and put in a cozy for 15 minutes. Fluff up and divide.

One pot method: Bring 3 cups water to a boil and turn off the stove. Add in the dry ingredients, stir well, cover tightly and let sit covered for 15 minutes. In cool temperatures use a pot cozy.

Serves 2

Notes: Top with grated cheese or fried onions after cooking. To make richer, add in a couple Tablespoons of butter to the hot water, before adding in the dry ingredients.

Chicken Florentine Mashers

In a sandwich or pint freezer bag:
3/4 cup instant mashed potatoes
2 Tbsp freeze-dried or dehydrated canned chicken
1 Tbsp dry milk
1 Tbsp dried crumbled spinach
2 tsp chicken gravy powder mix
1 tsp dried parsley

FBC method: Add 1 1/2 cups near boiling water to the freezer bag. Stir well, seal tightly and put in a cozy for 15 minutes.

Insulated mug method: In a large insulated mug add the dry ingredients and 1 1/2 cups boiling water. Stir well, cover tightly and let sit for 15 minutes.

One pot method: Bring 1 1/2 cups water to a boil and add in the dry ingredients. Stir well, cover tightly and let sit for 10 to 15 minutes. In cooler temperatures use a pot cozy.

Serves 1

Turkey and Gravy Mashers

In a sandwich or pint freezer bag:
3/4 cup instant mashed potatoes
1/4 cup freeze-dried turkey or dehydrated canned turkey
1 Tbsp dry milk
1 Tbsp diced dried shallots (or onions)
2 tsp turkey gravy powdered mix, preferably organic
1 tsp dried chives
1/4 tsp granulated garlic

FBC method: Add 1 1/2 cups near boiling water to the freezer bag. Stir well, seal tightly and put in a cozy for 15 minutes.

Insulated mug method: In a large insulated mug add the dry ingredients and 1 1/2 cups boiling water. Stir well, cover tightly and let sit for 15 minutes.

One pot method: Bring 1 1/2 cups water to a boil and add in the dry ingredients. Stir well, cover tightly and let sit for 10 to 15 minutes. In cooler temperatures use a pot cozy.

Serves 1

Note: Parmesan cheese sprinkled on top or powdered instant stuffing mix make great toppings. To powder the stuffing mix run it through a mini food chopper or blender.

Masher Patties

In a quart freezer bag:
1 Tbsp diced dried onion
2 Tbsp dry milk
2 Tbsp butter powder
3/4 cup instant mashed potatoes
1 cup diced nuts of choice

Also take:
2 Tbsp or 2 packets olive oil

FBC method: Add 1 cup near boiling water to the potatoes, stirring well. Seal tightly and let sit in a cozy for 10 minutes. Taste and add salt and pepper as desired.

Heat up 1 Tbsp oil in your pot and drop spoonfuls of the mixture into it carefully, cook till golden brown, turning once and flattening the patties. Add more oil as needed.

How many depends on how big yours are!

Notes: Add in grated cheese for more calories. A non-stick pot works best, allowing simple cleanup when done. BBQ sauce or salsa to dip the hot patties in is very tasty!

Cheesy Potatoes

In a quart freezer bag:
2 cups sliced dried potatoes

Cheese Sauce

In a sandwich bag:
2 Tbsp all-purpose flour
1/3 cup dry milk
1 tsp parsley
1/2 tsp onion powder
1/2 tsp dry mustard
1/4 tsp paprika
1/4 tsp ground black pepper
Salt, to taste

Also take:
2 Tbsp or 2 packets olive oil
4 ounces cheddar cheese, diced

Add potatoes and 4 cups water to a 2L pot, bring to a boil, simmer for 5 minutes and then let sit tightly covered for 15 minutes. Drain off water and stash in the quart freezer bag.

Add the oil to the dry ingredients in your pot and then slowly whisk in 1-cup water. Stir till thickened over a medium flame. Add in the cheese and take off the heat, stir in the potatoes.

Serves 2

Potato Curry Skillet

In a sandwich bag:
2 cups dried hash browns
2 tsp mild curry powder
1/2 tsp granulated garlic

Also take:
2 Tbsp or 2 packets olive oil

Add 1 1/3 cups water, the oil and dry ingredients in a nonstick pot and bring to a boil. Cook over a medium flame, stirring often, until the water is absorbed. Salt to taste, if desired.

Serves 2

Note: Pack in a small container of plain yogurt for topping. You can add diced onions, chives, black pepper, lemon juice – whatever you like – if you want to flavor it up. Yogurt carries well for the first two days or longer in cold weather.

Cheesy Hash Brown Skillet

In a quart freezer bag:
2 cups instant hash browns
1 Tbsp diced dried onions
1 Tbsp diced dried bell peppers
1/4 tsp ground black pepper

Also take:
2 to 3 ounces cheddar cheese
2 Tbsp or 2 packets olive oil

Add 2 cups near boiling water to the freezer bag, seal tightly, put in a cozy and let sit for at least 15 minutes to fully rehydrate.
Dice the cheese up and set aside.
Heat the oil over a medium flame in a large non-stick pot and add the potatoes in, stirring often, till golden brown.
Take off the stove and top with the cheese, stirring it in. Cover with the lid and let sit till melted, a couple minutes.

Serves 2

Scalloped Potatoes

In a sandwich bag:
1 cup dried potato slices
1 Tbsp diced dried onion
1 Tbsp diced dried carrots
1 tsp lower sodium chicken bouillon
1/4 tsp ground black pepper

In a snack size bag:
2 Tbsp dried bread crumbs
2 Tbsp shelf stable Parmesan cheese
1/2 tsp dried parsley

Also take:
3-ounce can of chicken

Add 1-cup water to the potato bag, seal tightly and let for 30 minutes to start the rehydration. Add the bag and the chicken to your pot with any broth, bring to a boil, take off the stove and let sit tightly covered for 15 minutes. Sprinkle the topping on and mix in.

Serves 1

Cheesy Scalloped Potatoes

In a sandwich bag:
1 cup dried potato slices
1/4 cup dry milk
1/4 cup cheddar cheese powder or cheese sauce powder
2 Tbsp diced dried onion
1/4 tsp dried rosemary, broken up
1/4 tsp ground black pepper

Add 1-cup water to the bag, sealing tightly. Let sit for 30 minutes to start the rehydration. Add the bag to your pot and bring to a boil, take off the stoves and let sit tightly covered for 15 minutes.

Serves 1

Stuffing Dishes

Chicken & Stuffing

In a sandwich bag:
3/4 cup freeze-dried mixed vegetables
2 Tbsp diced dehydrated onions
1 Tbsp low sodium chicken bouillon
1/2 tsp ground black pepper
1/4 tsp diced dried garlic

Also take:
1/4 cup shelf stable Parmesan cheese
6 to 8 ounce package instant stuffing mix
7-ounce pouch chicken

Put the chicken and dry ingredients into your pot with 3 cups water and bring to a boil. Add in the stuffing mix, tightly cover and turn off your stove and let sit for 5 minutes. Stir the stuffing and fold in the Parmesan cheese.

Serves 2

Notes: Use Stove Top brand instant stuffing or similar for best results.

Couscous Dishes

Curry Sauce Over Couscous

In a sandwich bag:
2 Tbsp dry milk
2 Tbsp all-purpose flour
1 Tbsp diced dried onions
1 tsp dried parsley
3/4 tsp curry powder
1/4 tsp salt

Take in a pint freezer bag:
3/4 cup couscous
1/4 tsp ginger powder

Add 1 cup near boiling water to the couscous and stir well. Seal tightly and put in a cozy for 10 minutes.

Meanwhile, add 1-cup water to your pot, add in the dry ingredients and stir well over high heat. Bring to a boil while stirring. Turn off the heat, cover tightly and let sit for five minutes. In cold temperatures insulate your pot in a pot cozy.

Serve the sauce over the couscous.

Serves 2

Alfredo Chicken & Pasta

In a sandwich bag:
1/3 cup couscous
1 Tbsp dried onion
1 Tbsp dry Alfredo mix (see dry mix section)
1 tsp dried parsley
1/4 tsp dried granulated garlic
1 Tbsp dry milk

Also take:
3-ounce can chicken breast
1 Tbsp shelf stable Parmesan cheese

One pot method:
Bring 1/2 cup water and the chicken to a boil in your pot. Turn off the stove, add in the dry ingredients and stir well. Put the lid on tightly and let sit for 10 minutes. Stir again and top with Parmesan cheese.

FBC method:
Add the chicken and 1/2 cup near boiling water. Stir well, seal tightly and put in a cozy for 15 minutes. Stir and top with Parmesan cheese.

Insulated mug method:
Add the chicken and ½ cup boiling water to the dry ingredients. Stir well, cover tightly and let sit for 15 minutes. Stir and top with Parmesan cheese.

Serves 1

Pizza In A Pot

In a sandwich bag:
2/3 cup couscous
1 Tbsp diced sun-dried tomato
1 Tbsp diced bell pepper
1 tsp dried Oregano
1 tsp dried Basil
1/4 tsp dried garlic

Also take:
1 Tbsp olive oil
1 4-ounce package sliced Pepperoni (shelf stable)
2 ounces Mozzarella cheese, diced

One pot method:
Add 1-cup water to your pot and bring to a boil. Turn off the stove and add in the dry ingredients, oil and pepperoni. Stir well, put the lid on tightly and let sit for 10 minutes. Meanwhile dice the cheese up. Top with the cheese and let sit for a minute.

FBC method:
Add the pepperoni, oil and 1 cup near boiling water. Stir well, seal tightly and put in a cozy for 15 minutes. Dice up the cheese, fold in and let sit for a minute.

Insulated mug method:
In a large mug add the pepperoni, oil and 1 cup boiling water to the dry ingredients. Stir well, cover tightly and let sit for 15 minutes. Dice up the cheese, fold in and let sit for a minute.

Serves 2.

Cherry Chicken Couscous

1 cup couscous
1/2 cup diced pitted dried unsweetened cherries
1 Tbsp diced dried onions
1/2 tsp diced dried garlic
1 tsp dried parsley
1 tsp True Lime powder
1 tsp low sodium chicken bouillon

Also take:
1 Tbsp or packet olive oil
1 5-ounce can or 7-ounce pouch chicken

Bring 1 1/2 cups water, oil and chicken with broth to a boil in your pot. Add in the dry ingredients, stir well, cover tightly and turn off the heat. Let sit for 10 minutes, fluff up.

Insulated mug method:
Add 1 1/2 cups boiling water, oil and chicken with broth to the dry ingredients in a large mug. Stir well, cover tightly and let sit for 10 minutes. Fluff up.

FBC method:
Add 1 1/2 cups near boiling water, oil and chicken with broth to the bag. Stir well, seal tightly and put in a cozy for 10 minutes. Fluff up.

Serves 2

Indian Spiced Chicken and Couscous

In a sandwich bag:
1/2 tsp turmeric
1/2 tsp ground fenugreek
1/2 tsp mustard seeds
1/2 tsp cayenne pepper
1/8 tsp ground fennel seed
1/4 tsp garlic powder
1/4 tsp ginger powder
1/4 tsp dried lemon zest
1 tsp low sodium bouillon
1 cup couscous

Also take:
1 7-ounce pouch chicken breast
1 Tbsp olive oil

One pot method:
Add 1 1/2 cups water, the chicken and oil to a boil in your pot. Turn the stove off and add the couscous. Stir, then cover tightly and let sit for 10 minutes.

FBC method:
Add the chicken, oil and 1 1/2 cups near boiling water. Stir well, seal tightly and put in a cozy for 15 minutes.

Serves 2

Cheesy Roast Beef Casserole

In a sandwich bag:
1 cup couscous
1 Tbsp diced dried onion
1 Tbsp diced sun-dried tomatoes
1 tsp low sodium beef bouillon
1/2 tsp diced dried garlic

Also take:
1 Tbsp olive oil
1 12-ounce can roast beef
1/4 cup shelf stable Parmesan cheese
Salt and pepper to taste

Open the roast beef and add it along with the broth, oil and 1-cup water to your pot. Bring to a boil. Turn off the heat and add in the dry ingredients. Stir well, seal tightly and let sit for 10 minutes. Fluff up and stir in the cheese. Season to taste.

Serves 2

Notes:
Canned roast beef you might ask? If you can find a good source of it, it is worth stocking up on. It is worth the extra weight. It has the taste and texture of long simmered stew beef. It can also be dehydrated, for lighter weight. Rehydrate, add to recipe and proceed.

Sun-Dried Tomato and Parmesan Couscous

In a sandwich bag:
1 cup couscous
1/4 cup diced sun-dried tomatoes
3 Tbsp toasted pine nuts
3 Tbsp shelf stable Parmesan cheese
1 Tbsp dried minced onion
1 Tbsp dried parsley
1 tsp dried oregano
1 tsp dried rosemary
1/4 tsp salt
1/4 tsp ground black pepper

Also take:
1 Tbsp or packet olive oil

In your pot bring 1 1/2 cups water and the oil to a boil. Add in the dry ingredients and stir well. Turn off the heat, cover tightly and let sit for 10 minutes. Fluff up before serving.

Insulated mug method:
Add 1 1/2 cups boiling water and the oil to the dry ingredients in your mug. Stir well and cover tightly and let sit for 10 minutes, fluff up.

FBC method:
Add 1 1/2 cups near boiling water and oil to the bag. Stir well, seal tightly and put in a cozy for 10 minutes. Fluff up.

Serves 2

Minted Chicken Couscous

1 cup couscous
1 Tbsp diced dried shallots
2 Tbsp dried mint leaves
1/4 tsp True Lime or 1 Tbsp lime juice

Also take:
1 Tbsp or packet olive oil
1 5-ounce can chicken

In your pot bring 1-cup water, the chicken with broth and oil to a boil. Add in the dry ingredients and stir well. Turn off the heat, cover tightly and let sit for 10 minutes. Fluff up.

Insulated mug method:
Add 1 cup boiling water, the chicken with any broth and oil to the dry ingredients in your mug. Stir well, cover tightly and let sit for 10 minutes. Fluff up.

FBC method:
Add 1 cup near boiling water, the chicken with any broth and oil to the bag. Stir well, seal tightly and put in a cozy for 10 minutes. Fluff up.

Curry Sauce over Couscous

In a freezer bag:
3/4 cup couscous

In a sandwich bag:
1/4 cup diced dried apples
1/4 cup raisins
2 tsp diced dried onion
2 tsp mild curry powder
1 tsp packed brown sugar

In a small bag:
1 Tbsp all-purpose flour

Also take:
1 Tbsp or packet olive oil
Salt to taste

Bring 1 cup water to a near boil. Add it to the couscous bag, stir well, seal tightly and put in a cozy for 10 minutes.

Heat the oil in your pot over a low flame and mix with the flour until smooth. Stir in 1 cup water and mix well, then add in the fruit and spice bag. Bring to a boil and then let sit tightly covered for 5 minutes.

Serve over the couscous.

Serves 2

Lime Curry Couscous

In a quart freezer or sandwich bag:
1/2 cup couscous
1/4cup sliced almonds
1/4 cup golden raisins
1 tsp mild curry powder
1/2 tsp True Lime© powder

In a small bag:
1/2 cup cooked and dehydrated chickpeas
2 Tbsp diced dried carrots

Also take:
1 Tbsp or packet olive oil

FBC method:
Add 1/2 cup cool water to the chickpea bag and seal. Let sit for 15 to 30 minutes to rehydyrate.
Bring 1 cup water to a near boil. Add it, the oil and the rehydrated chickpeas to the freezer bag. Seal tightly and put in a cozy for 15 minutes. Season to taste with salt and pepper, if desired.

One pot method:
Add 1/2 cup cool water to the chickpea bag and seal. Let sit for 15 to 30 minutes to rehydrate.
Add the oil, chickpeas and 1 cup water to your pot and bring to a boil. Turn off the heat and add in the dry ingredients. Cover tightly and let sit for 15 minutes. In cool temperatures use a pot cozy to insulate. Season to taste with salt and pepper, if desired.

Serves 2

Note:
Substitute one fresh small lime for the True Lime© powder, cut in half and squeeze over the cooked meal, stir in.

Single Serving Pasta Dishes

Florentine Tortellini

In a sandwich bag:
8 ounces spinach tortellini

In a sandwich bag:
1/4 cup tomato powder
2 Tbsp shelf stable Parmesan cheese
2 Tbsp diced dried spinach
1 Tbsp diced sun-dried tomatoes
1 tsp diced dried onion
1/2 tsp Italian seasoning
1/2 tsp sugar
1/4 tsp ground black pepper
1/8 tsp salt, or to taste

Also take 1 Tbsp or 1 packet olive oil
Additional Parmesan cheese if desired

At home:
Whirl the dry sauce ingredients in a blender till finely broken up.

Bring 4 cups water and the tortellini to a boil, cook for half the time on the package. Cover tightly and let sit for the other half. If in cooler temperatures insulate the pot. Drain and reserve 1 cup of the cooking water. Add it back to the pot along with the dry ingredients with the oil; stir till the sauce is smooth. Let sit for a couple minutes to hydrate.

Serves 2

One Pot Peppers and Tomatoes

In a sandwich bag:
4 ounces spaghetti, broken into third (7 minute cook time or less)
1/4 cup diced dried bell peppers
1/4 cup diced sun-dried tomatoes
1 Tbsp diced dried onions
2 tsp low sodium vegetable bouillon
1 tsp parsley
1/2 tsp granulated garlic
1 bay leaf

Also take 1 Tbsp or 1 packet olive oil

Bring 2 cups water, oil and the ingredients to a boil, lower the heat to a gentle boil and cook for time on pasta package, stirring often.
If desired season to taste with Parmesan cheese and or salt.

Serves 1

Creamy Broccoli Primavera

In a quart freezer bag:
4-ounces precooked and dehydrated pasta

In a sandwich bag:
1 1/2 Tbsp all-purpose flour
1/3 cup dry milk
2 Tbsp dried broccoli
Black pepper, to taste
1/4 tsp granulated garlic
1/4 tsp dried diced garlic
1/2 tsp dried chives
1/2 tsp red bell pepper flakes
1/2 tsp dried onions or shallots
1/8 tsp salt
2 Tbsp shelf stable Parmesan cheese

In a leak proof container:
1 1/2 Tbsp olive oil or 1 to 2 packets

Add near boiling water to just cover the pasta in its bag. Seal tightly and put in a cozy for 15 minutes. Drain any remaining water off.

Add the oil to the dry ingredients in a pan, and 1-cup water. Stir well with a whisk or spoon and cook till bubbling, then let sit till pasta is ready.

Combine the sauce with pasta, and if desired, sprinkle a little more Parmesan cheese on top.

Serves 1

Spicy Cashew Noodles

In a quart freezer bag:
1 3-ounce block ramen (no flavor packet)

In a sandwich bag:
3/4 cup unsalted cashews, ground to a powder
2 Tbsp cornstarch
1 tsp dried parsley
1 tsp dried onion
1/2 tsp dried celery flakes
1/4 tsp dried diced garlic
1/4 tsp salt
1/4-1/2 tsp red pepper flakes

Add 1 1/2 cups near boiling water to the ramen bag. Seal tightly and allow the ramen to soften, then put in a cozy.

Meanwhile in your pot add 2 1/2 cups water to the dry ingredients. Stir well and cook over high heat till the sauce thickens.

Turn off the heat and toss the noodles with the sauce.

Serves 1

Notes:
Works well with peanuts and with a touch of sesame oil.

Spicy Beef Lo Mein

In a quart freezer bag:
1 block ramen (toss flavor packet)
1/4 cup diced dried vegetables (put in what you like)
1 Tbsp "Beef" TVP or cooked and dehydrated hamburger

In a small bag take:
1/2 tsp diced dried garlic
1/4 tsp powdered dried ginger
1/4 tsp red chili pepper flakes
1/4 tsp dried chives

In a leak proof container take:
1 Tbsp or 1 packet olive oil
2 tsp or 1 to 2 packets low sodium soy sauce
1 tsp sesame oil

Add 1 1/2 cups near boiling water to the ramen bag. Put in a cozy for 5 minutes. Opening a tiny bit of the zipper, carefully drain off any remaining water.

Meanwhile in your pan add the oil bottle and heat over a medium flame if you can control it. As soon as hot and starting to sizzle add in the drained ramen bag and the dry seasonings. Using a heatproof utensil or tiny spatula start stirring and keep the pasta moving. It will need 2-3 minutes. Turn off the stove and keep stirring for a minute more. Serve up!

Serves 1

Lo Mein is an American "Chinese" dish that one can make however they like. It is cheap and easy to whip up and will stick to your ribs. Being a hybrid recipe you will need a pot that holds 3 or more cups.

Ramen in itself minus the 'flavor' packet is relatively low in sodium and works well in one pan meals as it doesn't need to be boiled first - it is precooked pasta. I used low sodium soy sauce, you may wish to use regular. If you don't like heat, leave the pepper flakes out.

One Pot Chicken & Veggies

In a sandwich bag:
4 ounces small pasta shapes
1 Tbsp diced dried tomatoes
1 Tbsp diced dried carrots
1 Tbsp diced dried shallots or onions
1 Tbsp diced dried spinach
1 1/2 tsp low sodium chicken bouillon
1/2 tsp chives
1/4 tsp dried garlic
1/4 tsp Thyme
1/4 tsp ground black pepper

Also bring:
1 7-ounce pouch of chicken
1 Tbsp (3 packets) shelf stable Parmesan cheese
2 packets soy sauce (2 tsp)

Bring the dry ingredients, chicken, soy sauce and 1 1/2 cups water to a boil in your pot. Cook, covered, on low heat (gently bubbling) for 7 minutes. Turn off heat and let sit for 5 minutes covered. Add in the cheese, stirring well.

Serves 1 large appetite, 2 smaller ones

Chickpea Spaghetti

In a sandwich bag:
4 ounces spaghetti (6 to 7 minute cook time or less), broken into thirds

In a small bag:
2 Tbsp cooked and dehydrated garbanzo beans
2 tsp low sodium chicken or vegetable bouillon
1/4 tsp diced dried garlic
1 tsp dried parsley
Pinch red pepper flakes
1/4 tsp fresh ground black pepper

In a small bag:
1/4 cup shelf stable Parmesan cheese

Also take:
1 Tbsp or 1 packet olive oil

Soak the contents of the bean bag and the oil for 10 minutes in your pot in 2 1/4 cups water. Bring to a boil, add in spaghetti and cook over a gentle boil for time on package or until al dente. (There will be broth remaining). Turn off your stove and add in the cheese, stirring well and let sit for a couple minutes to meld.
Salt to taste if desired.

Serves 1

Homemade "Box" Mac and cheese

In a sandwich bag:
1 cup macaroni pasta

Take:
2 Tbsp butter

In a small bag:
2 Tbsp dry milk
3 Tbsp cheddar cheese powder (dried finely grated cheese)

In your pot bring 3 cups water to a boil. Cook pasta according to package directions; drain carefully, leaving about 1/4 cup of water in the pot.
Add butter and melt using the heat of the noodles. Add milk and cheese and mix well.

Serves 1

Spicy Chicken Spaghetti

In a sandwich bag:
4 ounces thin spaghetti, broken into quarters
3 Tbsp crumbled dried mushrooms
1 Tbsp diced dried carrots
1 Tbsp diced dried onions
1 1/2 tsp low sodium chicken bouillon
1/4 tsp diced dried garlic
1/4 tsp red pepper flakes

Also take
1 5-ounce can or 7-ounce pouch of chicken
1-2 packets soy sauce (2-4 tsp)

Add 1 1/2 cups water, the chicken and pasta bag ingredients into your pot. Bring to a boil, put the lid on and turn down to low. Let it gently bubble for 7 minutes or so. Stir a couple times to keep the pasta moving. Turn off the heat and add in one packet of soy sauce. Let sit tightly covered for 5 minutes to meld. Taste to see if you need more soy sauce.

Serves 1

Veggie and Pasta Toss

In a sandwich bag put:
4 ounces of precooked and dehydrated pasta shapes
1/4 cup of sun dried tomatoes, minced
2 Tbsp dried broccoli
1/4 tsp granulated garlic

In camp boil 2 cups water with the pasta and vegetables. Let sit covered for 5 minutes. Drain excess water carefully. Add in the oil, cheese and nuts.

Mix in:
1 Tbsp or 1 packet olive oil
1-2 Tbsp shelf stable Parmesan cheese
1-2 Tbsp of pine nuts or shelled pistachio nuts

Serves 1

Chicken Tomato Pesto Shells

In a sandwich bag:
1/2 cup diced sun dried tomatoes
1 1/2 cups small shell pasta

In a small bag:
1/3 cup toasted pine nuts
1 packet dry pesto mix
¼ cup shelf stable Parmesan cheese

Also take
1 Tbsp olive oil, in a leak proof bottle
1 5-ounce can or 7-ounce pouch of chicken

Bring 3 cups water to a boil and add in pasta bag contents. Cook for time on pasta package. Drain pasta carefully reserving ¼ cup pasta water in a cup. Add back in two Tablespoons of the water to the pan. Drizzle in the oil, the pesto bag contents and the chicken. Heat through on low till bubbly. If needed, add in more of the reserved water.

Serves 1.

Pasta Primavera

In a sandwich bag put:
4 ounces precooked and dehydrated pasta
1/4 cup freeze-dried mixed vegetables

Also take:
1 Tbsp olive oil or butter
2 Tbsp shelf stable Parmesan cheese
Seasonings of choice

In camp boil 2 cups water with the pasta and vegetables. Cover and let sit for 5 minutes. Drain carefully. Toss the oil with the pasta, then the cheese and any seasonings desired.
Serves 1.

Chili Mac

In a sandwich bag:
4 ounces small macaroni cooked and dehydrated
1/3 cup diced sun-dried tomatoes
1/4 cup cooked and dehydrated black beans
3 tablespoons dry milk
3 tablespoons freeze-dried corn
2 tablespoons diced dried bell peppers
3 tsp chili powder
1 tsp diced dried onion
3/4 tsp dried celery
1/2 tsp cornstarch
1/4 tsp granulated garlic
1/4 tsp sugar
2 Tbsp tomato sauce powder

Also take:
2-ounces cheddar cheese

In your pot add 2 1/2 cups water and the dry ingredients. Bring to a boil, stirring well. Cover tightly; turn off the heat and let sit in a pot cozy for 10 minutes.

Stir and top with cheese.

Serves 1.

Kiddie Mac & Cheese

In a sandwich bag:
1 cup uncooked small macaroni
½ cup freeze-dried green peas

In a second sandwich bag:
1/4 cup dry milk
1 Tbsp dried parsley
1 tsp dried chives
1/4 tsp granulated garlic
1/4 tsp dry mustard powder
Black pepper to taste

Also take:
4 ounces cheddar cheese
1 3-ounce pouch of tuna

Dice up the cheese and set aside.

Bring 3 cups water to a boil in your pot. Add in the pasta and cook for time on pasta package. Carefully drain off most of the remaining water, reserving ½ cup.

Add in the dry bag of ingredients and the cheese to the pasta, stirring over low heat. Add in reserved water as needed to make the sauce. As it starts to melt, add in the tuna and warm through.

Serves 1

Salmon With Green Beans

In a sandwich bag:
4 ounces twist shaped pasta
1/2 cup freeze-dried green beans

Also take:
1 foil pouch salmon steak (or tuna steak)
1 Tbsp or 1 packet olive oil
2 Tbsp shelf stable Parmesan cheese
1 packet True Lemon or 1 packet lemon juice
Black pepper to taste

In your pot bring 3 cups water to a boil and add the pasta/beans. Cook for time on pasta package. Turn off the stove and carefully drain off the water when done.
Add in the oil and salmon and stir to combine. Add in the True Lemon and Parmesan, tossing to coat. Add fresh ground black pepper to taste and salt if desired.

Serves 1

French Onion Noodle Bowl

1 3-ounce package ramen (toss the flavor packet)

Pack in a small bag:
3 Tbsp diced dried onion
2 Tbsp "Beef" flavored TVP or cooked and dehydrated or freeze-dried hamburger
2 tsp low sodium beef bouillon powder
1 tsp celery flakes
1/4 tsp ground black pepper

Pack in a small bag:
1/4 cup instant stuffing mix

Add 2 cups water to your pot. Add in the bag containing the onions and beef, let sit for 5 minutes to rehydrate.

Bring the water to a boil, add in the ramen and cook on a gentle boil for 3 minutes. Taste and add salt if desired. Pull off the heat and top with the stuffing mix.

Serves 1.

Note:
If you cannot find baked ramen you can use Chuka Soba noodles instead. They come often in 8-ounce packages, break off half. Follow cooking time on the package.

Pesto For One

In a sandwich bag:
4 ounces small pasta shapes (cooking time less than 7 minutes)

In a second bag:
1/4 cup toasted and ground pine nuts
1/4 cup shelf stable Parmesan cheese
2 Tbsp dried basil
1/4 tsp diced dried garlic
1/4 tsp ground black pepper

Also take 1 Tbsp or 1 packet extra virgin olive oil

One pot method:
Bring 2 cups water to a boil, add in the pasta and cook for time on package. Drain off remaining water carefully, reserving 1/4 cup in your mug.
Add the oil and seasoning mix to the pot, stirring well. Add in water as needed to make a smooth sauce.

Serves 1

Trailhead's Thai Tom Yum Noodle Bowl

In a sandwich bag:
1 package ramen (toss the flavor packet)
1 Tbsp coconut cream powder
1 Tbsp diced dried carrots
1 Tbsp diced dried onions
2 tsp low sodium chicken bouillon
1/2 tsp dried ground ginger
1/4 - 1/2 tsp red pepper flakes
1/4 tsp True Lime powder or bring 1 small lime

Also take 1 5-ounce can chicken

Bring 2 cups water and the chicken with broth to a boil. Add in the dry
ingredients. Return to a boil and cook on a gentle boil for 3 minutes.
If using a fresh lime, squeeze in. Add salt to taste, if desired.

Serves 1.

Note:
If you cannot find baked ramen you can use Chuka Soba noodles
instead. They come often in 8-ounce packages, break off half. Follow
cooking time on the package.

Pasta Dishes For Two

Italian Tuna Spaghetti

In a sandwich bag:
8 ounces angel hair pasta, broken into thirds
1/4 cup diced sun-dried tomatoes

In a small bag:
1 tsp oregano
1/2 tsp granulated garlic
1 tsp dried basil
1/4 cup shelf stable parmesan cheese

Also take:
3-ounce pouch of tuna
2 Tbsp or 2 packets olive oil

Bring 3 cups water to a boil in your pot, add the pasta and cook for
time on pasta package. Turn off the heat and drain the water off
carefully

Add tuna, oil and contents of the cheese and spice package. Toss and
serve.

Serves 2

Trail Carbonara

In a sandwich bag:
8 ounces spaghetti, broken into thirds

In a sandwich bag:
1/4 cup shelf stable bacon
1 Tbsp dry parsley
1/2 cup shelf stable Parmesan cheese
1/2 tsp ground black pepper

In a snack bag:
1/4 cup dry egg mix

Also take:
2 Tbsp or 2 packets olive oil

Mix the powdered eggs with 6 Tbsp cold water in the bag, seal tightly and shake to dissolve, set aside.
Meanwhile, bring 6 cups of water to a boil in a 2 Liter pot. Cook spaghetti for time on package, and then drain carefully. Toss the hot pasta with the oil, egg mix and the seasoning mix over a low flame till coated and cooked through. Season to taste with salt if desired.

Serves 2

Notes: We recommend Ova Easy egg mix, it is the closest to fresh that we have found. Find online through www.packitgourmet.com

Lemony Spinach Linguini With Salmon

In a sandwich bag:
8 ounces spinach linguine, broken into thirds

In a small bag:
1/2 tsp granulated garlic
1 tsp dried dill
1/2 tsp dried lemon zest
3 packets True Lemon powder or 1 lemon or 3 packets lemon juice
1/4 cup shelf stable Parmesan cheese

Also take:
1/4 cup olive oil
3-ounce foil pouch salmon

Bring 3 cups water to a boil in your pot, add in the pasta and cook for time on pasta package. Turn off the heat and drain the water off carefully, reserving a 1/4 cup. Fold in the salmon, toss with the oil and seasonings. Add in reserved water as needed for sauce.

Serves 2

Peas and Pasta

In a sandwich bag:
8 ounces small pasta shapes
1/3 cup freeze-dried peas
1/3 cup freeze-dried ham, canned and dehydrated ham or 'ham' TVP
1/3 cup crumbled dried mushrooms

In a snack bag:
2 Tbsp dry milk
1 1/2 Tbsp all-purpose flour
1 Tbsp butter powder
1/4 tsp dried basil
1/4 cup shelf stable Parmesan cheese

Bring to a boil 3 cups of water and add in the pasta bag. Cook for time on pasta package. Do not drain. When done add in the dry sauce bag and stir until creamy. Season to taste with salt and pepper if desired.

Serves 2

Chicken a la King

In a sandwich bag:
2 cups thin egg noodles
1/2 cup freeze-dried peas

In a sandwich bag:
1/4 cup dry milk
3 Tbsp flour
2 Tbsp butter powder
1 Tbsp dried parsley

Also take:
7-ounce pouch chicken

Bring 2 cups water to a boil and gently cook the pasta bag for time on package. Do not drain the noodles. Add in the chicken and sauce bag, stirring well till creamy and warmed through.

Serves 2 to 3

Spicy Italian Pasta

In a sandwich bag:
8 ounces small pasta shapes (cooking time under 7 minutes)
1/3 cup diced sun-dried tomatoes
1/4 cup crumbled dried mushrooms
1 Tbsp dried or freeze-dried sliced olives

In a small bag:
1 Tbsp Italian herb blend
1/4 to 1/2 tsp red pepper flakes
1/4 cup shelf stable parmesan cheese

Also take:
1 Tbsp or 1 packet olive oil
1 packet shelf stable pepperoni

Bring 3 cups water to boil in your pot. Add the pasta and vegetables and cook for time on pasta package. Turn off the heat and drain the water off carefully. Toss with the olive oil and pepperoni. Add in the seasoning and cheese bag and toss to combine.

Serves 2

Lemon Pecan Pasta Toss

In a sandwich bag:
8 ounces angel hair pasta, broken into thirds

In a small bag:
1/2 tsp ground nutmeg
1/4 tsp ground black pepper
2 packets True Lemon powder or 2 lemon juice packets
1/4 cup shelf stable Parmesan cheese
1/4 cup diced toasted pecans

Also take:
1/4 cup olive oil

Bring 3 cups water in your pot to a boil, add in the angel hair and cook for time on pasta package. Turn off the heat and drain the water off carefully. Toss pasta with the olive oil and the seasonings and cheese. Salt to taste if desired.

Serves 2

Homemade Mac and cheese

In a sandwich bag:
8 ounces small pasta shapes (cooking time under 7 minutes)

In a small bag:
1/4 cup dry milk
1 Tbsp dried parsley
1 Tbsp dried chives
1/2 tsp dried diced garlic

Also take:
4 ounces cheese of choice

Dice the cheese up.
Meanwhile, bring 3 cups water to a boil in your pot. Add pasta and cook for time on pasta package. Turn off the heat and drain the water off carefully, reserving 1/2 cup water. Add in dry milk mix and cheese. Stir well over low heat, till melted. Add in reserved water as needed to make a smooth sauce.

Serves 2

Apricot and Rosemary Pasta

In a sandwich bag:
8 ounces small pasta shapes (cooking time under 7 minutes)

In a snack bag:
1 cup diced dried apricots
1 tsp dried rosemary, crumbled
1 tsp diced dried garlic

Also take:
2 Tbsp or 2 Packets olive oil
3/4 cup dry white wine

Also take:
Ground black pepper and salt, to taste

Bring to boil 6 cups water in a 2 Liter pot. Cook pasta for time on package drain and set aside in a clean freezer bag or in a bowl. Heat the oil in your pot and add the garlic, rosemary and apricots. Heat through and add in the wine. Bring to a simmer and toss with the cooked pasta. Add pepper and salt to taste.

Serves 2

Notes: You can find wine often in small servings, in shelf stable packaging. These packages keep the wine fresh and flatten down after using. If you are not a wine drinker, substitute broth.

Fall Harvest pasta

In a sandwich bag:
8 ounces small pasta (cooking time under 7 minutes)
1/4 cup crumbled dried mushrooms
1/4 cup cooked and dehydrated hamburger or 'beef' TVP

In a small bag:
1/2 tsp dried diced garlic
1/3 cup chopped toasted walnuts
1 1/2 tsp dry parsley
2 Tbsp shelf stable Parmesan cheese

Also take:
1/4 cup or 4 packets olive oil

Bring 3 cups water to a boil in your pot. Add the pasta bag contents and cook for time on pasta package. Turn off the heat and drain carefully.

Toss the pasta with the seasonings and oil.

Serves 2

Pasta Alfredo

In a sandwich bag:
8 ounces small pasta shapes (cooking time under 7 minutes)

Take:
2 Tbsp or 2 packets olive oil

In a small bag:
1/2 tsp granulated garlic
1/2 tsp dried dill
1/4 tsp ground pepper
2 Tbsp all-purpose flour

In a small bag:
1/3 cup dry milk
1/2 cup shelf stable parmesan cheese

Bring 3 cups water to a boil in your pot, add in the pasta and cook for time on pasta package. Turn off the heat and drain the water off carefully. Stash the pasta in a bowl or freezer bag. In your pot, warm the oil up till hot. Lower the heat to medium and add in the flour bag, stirring well till smooth. Slowly add 1-cup water, stirring until thick. Add in milk bag, and stir until blended. Turn off the heat and toss the pasta in to coat.

Serves 2

Note: If in a low water area, reserve the pasta cooking water and use it in your sauce.

Herbed Chicken Pasta

In a quart bag:
8 ounces angel hair or thin spaghetti (break in thirds)

In a small sandwich bag:
1 Tbsp dried parsley
1 Tbsp dried chives
1 tsp dry celery flakes
1 tsp granulated garlic
1/8 tsp ground black pepper
Pinch of red pepper flakes
1/4 cup shelf stable parmesan cheese

Also take:
1 Tbsp or 1 packet olive oil
7-ounce pouch chicken

Add the dry pasta to 4 cups water and bring to a boil in your pot. Cook for time on pasta package. Turn off the heat and drain the water off carefully. Toss with the oil, herbs, drained chicken and cheese. If desired heat through on very low heat for a minute or two.

Serves 2

Swiss Mac & Cheese

In a sandwich bag:
3 Tbsp all-purpose flour
1/2 cup dry milk
2 tsp mustard powder
1 Tbsp dried parsley
1 tsp granulated garlic
1/4 tsp black pepper

In a second sandwich bag:
8 ounces small shell pasta (cooking time under 7 minutes)
1/3 cup diced sun-dried tomatoes

Also take:
5 ounces Swiss cheese

Cut the cheese into very small chunks.

Bring 3 1/2 cups water to boil in your pot. Add pasta and tomatoes and cook for time on pasta package. When done, turn off the heat. Do not drain. Stir in the dry ingredients, then most of the cheese (reserve a bit for topping). Stir until the cheese melts. Serve and top with the reserved cheese.

Serves 2

Note: This recipe produces a lot of sauce, so make sure to have some crusty bread or rolls for mopping up the sauce!

Herb & Pepper Smoked Salmon Pasta

In a sandwich bag:
8 ounces small pasta (cooking time under 7 minutes)
1/3 cup diced sun-dried tomatoes
1/4 cup crumbled dried mushrooms

In a second sandwich bag:
1 Tbsp Italian herb
1/2 tsp red pepper flakes
1/4 cup shelf stable Parmesan cheese

Also take:
3 ounces smoked salmon (in shelf stable packaging)
1 Tbsp or 1 packet olive oil

Bring 4 cups of water to a boil in your pot. Add the pasta bag contents and cook for time on pasta package. Turn off the heat and drain the water off carefully. Toss with the olive oil, seasoning bag and salmon. Warm through if needed on low heat.

Serves 2

Seaside Mac & Cheese

In a sandwich bag put:
8 ounces uncooked small pasta (cooking time under 7 minutes)

In a second sandwich bag put:
1/4 cup dry milk
1 Tbsp dried parsley
1 tsp dried chives
1/4 tsp granulated garlic
1/4 tsp dry mustard powder
Black pepper to taste

Also take:
4 ounces cheese of choice, diced
1 can clams
2 Tbsp shelf stable bacon

Bring 4 cups water to a boil in your pot, add the pasta and cook for time on pasta package. Turn off the heat and drain most of the water off carefully. Add in the dry bag of ingredients and the cheese. Turn the stove on to low and start stirring. As it starts to melt, add in the clams, with clam juice, and warm thru. Top with the bacon.

Serves 2

Green Tofu Curry With Rice Noodles

In a small bag:
2 tsp Thai green curry paste

In a small bag:
1 Tbsp brown sugar
1 1.75-ounce packet coconut cream powder
1 packet True Lime© powder
1 Tbsp dried cilantro

In a quart freezer bag:
6 ounces thin rice noodles
1/4 cup diced dried carrots
1 Tbsp diced dried onion

Also take:
12-ounce package shelf stable firm tofu (you can use plain or flavored)

Warm up two cups water to hot but not boiling. Cover the rice noodles with the hot water and let sit for time on package (usually around 5 minutes).

Meanwhile, chop tofu into small cubes. In your pot, combine curry paste and coconut bag with 1 cup water and bring to boil. Stir in tofu and cook till heated through. Drain the rice noodles and add in. Toss to coat and let heat through again on low.

Serves 2

Notes: Mae Ploy is a good brand for the curry paste. It can be found in many grocery stores now in small tubs. It is fine to carry with you in your pack, just make sure when you repack it that it won't leak on accident. For the water used in the curry sauce, you can use the leftover water from your rice noodles.
For a first night dinner, carry baked and flavored tofu.

Citrus Forest Spaghetti

In a sandwich bag:
8 ounces thin spaghetti, broken into thirds

In a sandwich bag:
1/2 cup shelf stable Parmesan cheese
1/4 cup toasted pine nuts
2 packets True Lemon Powder or 2 packets lemon juice

Also bring:
2 Tbsp or 2 packets olive oil
Salt and pepper, to taste

Bring 3 cups water to a boil in your pot, add in the pasta and cook for time on pasta package. Turn off the heat and drain the water off carefully, leaving about 2 Tablespoons water behind. Toss with the oil and seasoning and cheese bag.

Serves 2

Herbed Salmon Noodles

In a sandwich bag:
8 ounces small pasta shapes (cooking time under 7 minutes)

In a small bag:
1/4 cup shelf stable Parmesan cheese
1 tsp dried celery flakes
1 tsp dried parsley
1/2 tsp dried thyme
1/2 tsp diced dried garlic
1/4 tsp ground black pepper
Pinch red pepper flakes to taste

Also take:
3-ounce pouch of wild salmon
1 to 2 Tbsp or 1 to 2 packets olive oil

Bring 3 cups water to a boil in your pot. Add the pasta and cook for time on pasta package. Turn off the heat and drain the water off carefully. Add the oil, salmon, herbs and toss to combine.

Serves 2

Pasta Alfredo with Salmon & Corn

In a snack bag:
1 packet dry Alfredo sauce mix
1/4 cup dry milk
2 Tbsp shelf stable Parmesan cheese
1 tablespoon dried basil
1 pinch ground black pepper

In a sandwich bag:
8 ounces small shaped pasta
1 cup freeze-dried corn

Also take:
4 ounces smoked salmon
1 Tbsp or 1 packet olive oil

Bring 4 cups water to a boil in your pot. Add in pasta bag contents and cook for time on pasta package. Drain pasta, reserving 1 cup water. Add dry ingredients to pasta, slowly adding in 3/4 cup of the reserved water and oil. Stir well, placing pot over low heat till bubbly and thick. Add rest of water if needed. Take off heat and add salmon, stirring in well.

Serves 2

Note: See the Dry Mixes and Seasoning section for a DIY Alfredo sauce mix.

Mushroom and Tomato Pesto Orzo

In a sandwich bag:
8 ounces orzo pasta
2 Tbsp sun-dried tomatoes
2 Tbsp crumbled dried mushrooms

In a snack bag:
1 Tbsp pine nuts
1 Tbsp dry pesto mix
2 Tbsp or 4 packets shelf stable Parmesan cheese

Also take:
1 Tbsp or 1 packet olive oil

Add 2 cups water and the pasta bag to your pot and bring to a boil. Lower heat and cook bubbling gently until done, follow time on pasta package. Turn off heat. Drain off nearly all the water, leaving about a Tablespoon in the pan. Drizzle in oil, add pesto bag and stir till blended.

Serves 2

Note: See the Dry Mixes and Seasoning section for a DIY dry pesto mix.

Curried Beef & Noodles

In a sandwich bag:
2 ounces diced beef jerky
1 Tbsp diced dried carrots
1 Tbsp diced dried onions
1 Tbsp crumbled dried mushrooms
1 Tbsp golden raisins
6 ounces thin spaghetti, broken into thirds

In a second bag:
1 packet (about 1.75 ounces) coconut cream powder
1 Tbsp mild curry powder
1 tsp low sodium beef bouillon
1/4 tsp diced dried garlic

Bring 3 cups water and the first bag's ingredients to a boil in your pot. Turn down the heat and cook gently boiling for time on pasta package. Carefully drain the pasta, reserving the pasta water into a bowl or mug. Add back in 1 cup of the water along with the second bag's ingredients and mix well.

Return to stove over low heat, and stir until mixed and bubbling. Add in more of the reserved pasta water as needed to produce a creamy sauce. (Sauce will thicken as it cools) Turn the stove off and cover your pot tightly. Let sit 5 minutes.

Serves 2

Pasta With Clam Sauce

In a sandwich bag:
6 oz angel hair or thin spaghetti pasta, broken into thirds

Also take
1 can clams
1 Tbsp or 1 packet olive oil

In a small bag:
1/4 cup shelf stable Parmesan cheese
1/2 tsp diced dried garlic
1/2 tsp red pepper flakes
1/2 tsp Italian herb
Salt and pepper to taste

Bring 3 cups water to a boil in your pot and cook for time on pasta package. Turn off the heat and drain the water off carefully. Add olive oil, clams with juices and heat over medium until it just starts to boil. Turn the heat off and toss the pasta with the Parmesan cheese. Add salt and pepper to taste if desired.

Serves 2

Garden Marinara

In a sandwich bag:
6 ounces small pasta shapes
2 Tbsp crumbled dried mushrooms
1/4 cup freeze-dried mixed vegetables

In a pint freezer bag:
1/4 cup tomato powder
1/2 tsp Italian seasoning
1/2 tsp sugar
1/4 tsp diced dried garlic
1/4 tsp ground black pepper
Pinch of salt

Also take:
2 Tbsp or 4 packets shelf stable Parmesan cheese

Bring 5 cups water to a boil in your pot. Take out 1 cup of it. Slowly add water to the tomato mix. Stir in till sauce reaches the texture you like, you will need at least 3/4 cup water; adding more will produce a thinner sauce. Seal the bag tightly and rest in a cozy.

Meanwhile, add the pasta and vegetables to the rest of the water in the pot. Boil gently for time on pasta package. Turn off heat and drain carefully. Add the prepared sauce, Parmesan cheese and if desired, a drizzle of olive oil. Toss together.

Serves 2

Artichoke Salmon Pasta

In a sandwich bag:
8 ounces thin spaghetti, broken into thirds.

In a snack bag:
1/4 cup Italian seasoned bread crumbs
1/4 shelf stable Parmesan cheese

In a sandwich bag:
14 ounce can quartered artichoke hearts, drained (non-oil type)
1 Tbsp capers, drained (non-oil type)

Also take:
3-ounce foil pouch smoked salmon
2 Tbsp or 2 packets extra virgin olive oil

Bring 4 cups water to a boil in your pot (2L size recommended). Add in the pasta and cook for time on pasta package. Turn off the heat and drain the water off carefully.
Add in the artichokes and capers, salmon and oil, mixing in well.
Return to your stove and on very low heat carefully warm up for a few seconds. Turn off stove and add in the cheese/bread crumbs. Stir to blend.

Serves 2 large appetites or 3 small ones

Notes: Capers can be dehydrated, soak in cool water separately before adding in.

Beef Stroganoff

In a sandwich bag:
8 ounces egg noodles
1/4 pound beef jerky, chopped into tiny pieces
2 tsp onion flakes
2 tsp paprika
2 Tbsp crumbled dried mushrooms
3/4 tsp tomato powder
2 Tbsp cream of mushroom soup dry mix
1/4 cup instant mashed potatoes

In a small bag:
1/4 cup + 2 tablespoons of sour cream powder
1/2 tsp dry parsley

Pour contents of jerky bag into medium pot and add 1 3/4 cups water. Bring to boil, and then simmer for 15 minutes, stirring occasionally. Add more water if needed. Cook egg noodles in separate pot following package directions. Drain, and put the stroganoff pot on heat, add sour cream mix but do not boil. Serve over hot noodles.

Serves 2

Note: Find sour cream powder and dry cream of mushroom soup online.

Tagliatelle Puttanesca

In a leak proof container:
2 Tbsp anchovy paste
2 Tbsp extra virgin olive oil
3 Tbsp tomato paste
1/2 tsp granulated garlic
1/2 tsp white sugar
1 tsp balsamic vinegar
1 Tbsp capers, rinsed and drained

In a sandwich bag:
12 ounces fettuccini pasta, broken into thirds

In a small bag:
3 Tbsp Parmesan cheese

Also take:
Freshly ground pepper to taste

Refrigerate the sauce mixture until leaving for trip. For extended storage take a freezer bag and fill with ice, wrap the container in a small bag, then insert into the freezer bag. Use sauce within 24 hours in hotter temperatures, 48 hours in cooler temperatures.

Bring 4 cups water to a boil in your pot and cook pasta for time on package. Carefully drain any remaining water and stir sauce in. Sprinkle with the Parmesan and pepper to taste.

Serves 2

Spicy Chicken Spaghetti

In a sandwich bag put:
4 ounces thin spaghetti, broken into quarters
3 Tbsp crumbled dried mushrooms
1 Tbsp diced dried carrots
1 Tbsp diced dried onions
1 1/2 tsp low sodium chicken bouillon
1/4 tsp diced dried garlic
1/4 tsp red pepper flakes

Also take
5-ounce can or 7-ounce pouch of chicken
1 to 2 packets or 2 to 4 tsp soy sauce

Add 1 1/2 cups water, the chicken and pasta bag ingredients into your pot. Bring to a boil, put the lid on and turn down to low. Let it gently bubble for 7 minutes or so. Stir a couple times to keep the pasta moving. Turn off the heat and add in one packet of soy sauce. Let sit tightly covered for 5 minutes to meld. Taste to see if you need more soy sauce.

Serves 1 to 2 (A very hungry hiker could eat the whole recipe, normal appetites two.)

Mexi Mac N' Cheese

In a sandwich bag:
Macaroni from 6 ounce box of organic mac n' cheese
1/4cup freeze-dried corn
1/4 cup diced sun-dried tomatoes
1/4 cup diced dried bell peppers
2 Tbsp 'beef' TVP or cooked and dehydrated hamburger

In a snack bag:
Cheese sauce packet contents
1 Tbsp dry milk

Also take:
3 Tbsp or 3 packets olive oil or butter
1/2 cup salsa (a single serving tub) or equivalent dried
2 ounces cheddar, co-jack or pepper-jack cheese

In your pot bring 4 cups water to a boil. Add in the pasta bag and cook for time on package (usually 7 minutes). Turn off the stove.
Carefully drain off most of the water, leaving behind 1/4 cup pasta water.
Mix in the oil (or butter) along with the sauce ingredients. Once blended, add in the salsa. Cover tightly and dice the cheese up. Stir in the cheese and let sit till melty.

Serves 2

Pasta Faux-Carbonara

In a sandwich bag:
1/2 cup shelf stable Parmesan cheese
3 Tbsp all-purpose flour
2/3 cup dry milk
1 Tbsp butter powder
1 Tbsp dried parsley
1/4 tsp salt
1/4 tsp ground black pepper
1/4 tsp diced dried garlic

In a sandwich bag:
2 Tbsp diced dried shallots or onions
8 ounces small pasta shapes (cooking time under 7 minutes)

Also take:
2 ounces shelf stable bacon or 'bacon' TVP

In your pot bring 4 cups water to a boil. Add the pasta in and cook for time on package. Drain carefully and reserve 1/2 cup pasta water. Add in the dry ingredients, mixing into the pasta. Slowly add in the reserved water. Cook over a low flame till it starts to thicken. Stir in the bacon and take off the heat. Top with more cheese if desired.

Serves 2

Spaghetti & Clams

In a sandwich bag:
1/2 tsp diced dried garlic
1 tsp red pepper flakes
6 oz angel hair or thin spaghetti pasta, broken into thirds

Also take
1 can of clams
1 Tbsp or 1 packet olive oil
1/2 cup shelf-stable Parmesan cheese
Salt and pepper

Bring 3 cups water to a boil in your pot, cook pasta until done and drain.
Add olive oil, clams with juices and heat until it just starts to boil. Turn the heat off and toss the pasta with the Parmesan cheese. Add salt and pepper to taste if desired.

Serves 2

Note: You can use shelf stable cheese, for best flavor pack in a piece of aged Parmesan or Romano cheese and grate it with a small backpacking grater, it is worth the weight for this recipe.

Tuna and Basil Penne

In a sandwich bag:
8 ounces small penne pasta (cooking time under 7 minutes)

Also take:
3-ounce pouch Albacore tuna
3 Tbsp extra virgin olive oil (or 3 packets)
1/4 tsp dried diced garlic
1 lemon juice packet or 1 packet True Lemon powder or 1 small fresh lemon
1 Tbsp dried lemon zest
1/4 cup packed fresh basil leaves, chopped
Salt and pepper, if desired

Bring 4 cups of water to a boil in your pot, add in the pasta and cook for time on package.
Open the tuna pouch and combine the tuna with everything but the pasta and season to taste.
Drain the pasta carefully when done, and then toss with the tuna mixture to combine.

Serves 2

Notes: Carry fresh basil? Yes! Just wrap it in a lightly damp paper towel, in a sandwich bag. Yes, you can use dried, but it will not taste the same. If you must use dried, use 1 to 2 teaspoons.

Pistachio Pasta Toss

In a sandwich bag:
8 ounces small shaped pasta (cooking time under 7 minutes)
1/4 cup diced sun-dried tomatoes
2 Tbsp diced dried broccoli

Also take:
1/4 tsp granulated garlic

1 Tbsp or 1 packet olive oil
1 to 2 Tbsp or 2 to 4 packets shelf stable Parmesan cheese
1 to 2 Tbsp shelled pistachio nuts

Bring 2 cups water to a boil in your pot, add in the pasta and
vegetables. Cook for time on pasta package. Drain excess water
carefully. Add in the oil, cheese and nuts and toss.

Serves 2

Spaghetti with Tuna & Lemon Breadcrumbs

In a sandwich bag:
8 ounces spaghetti, broken into thirds
3 Tbsp freeze-dried or dehydrated sliced olives

Also take:
1 Tbsp or 1 packet olive oil
3 Tbsp lemon juice (3 packets or 1 lemon)
3-ounce pouch Albacore tuna

In a small bag:
1/4 cup seasoned breadcrumbs
1 tsp dry lemon zest

In your pot bring 4 cups water to boil. Add in the pasta and olives and cook for time on package, drain carefully reserving 1/2 cup of the pasta water. Add in the oil, lemon juice and tuna and toss to combine. Sprinkle with breadcrumb mixture and toss again.

Serves 2

One Pot Pesto

In a large bag:
12 ounces small pasta shapes (cook time under 7 minutes)
1 cup freeze-dried green beans

Also take:
1 packet pesto powder sauce mix
4.5-ounce can tuna in olive oil (with pop-top)

In a small bag:
1/4 cup shelf stable Parmesan cheese

Bring 4 cups water to a boil in your pot, add in the pasta and cook for time on package. When done reserve the water called for on the pesto package and then drain off the pasta carefully.
Add the tuna with oil, the reserved water and the pesto mix, blending well. Heat over a low flame if desired. Toss with the Parmesan cheese.

Serves 2 to 3

Note: See the Dry Mixes and Seasonings section for a DIY pesto mix.

Double Peanut Noodles

In a large bag:
12 ounces small pasta shapes (cook time under 7 minutes)
2 Tbsp diced dried shallots or onions
¾ tsp red pepper flakes

Also take:
7-ounce pouch chicken breast
1/2 cup peanut butter

In a leak proof bottle:
1 Tbsp lower sodium soy sauce
2 tsp sesame oil
2 Tbsp rice vinegar

In a small bag:
2 Tbsp chopped peanuts

Bring 4 cups water to a boil, cook pasta for time on package. Drain carefully.
Meanwhile in a clean sandwich bag add 1-cup cool water to the peanut butter along with the sauce ingredients. Seal tightly and shake till mixed up.
Toss the hot pasta with the sauce; add in the chicken and the nuts.
Heat over low heat if desired.

Serves 2 to 3

Chicken and Peas

In a large bag:
12 ounces small pasta shapes (cook time under 7 minutes)
3/4 cup freeze-dried green peas
1/4 cup diced sun-dried tomatoes

Also take:
4 lower sodium broth sticks or 4 tsp low sodium chicken bouillon
7 ounce pouch chicken breast
1 Tbsp or 1 packet extra virgin olive oil
4 packets soy sauce, lower sodium preferably

In a small bag:
1/4 cup shelf stable Parmesan cheese

In a large pot bring 4 1/2 cups water to a boil, along with the broth concentrate and oil. Add in the pasta, vegetables and chicken. Bring back to a boil and cook for time on package. Turn off the stove, stir in the soy sauce, then the Parmesan cheese, then let sit for a couple minutes to thicken up.

Serves 2 to 3

Sesame Noodles

In a snack size bag:
1/2 cup diced dried carrots
1/4 cup dried or freeze-dried green peas

In a sandwich bag:
8 ounces spaghetti, broken in half

In a leak-proof bottle:
2 Tbsp lower sodium soy sauce
2 tsp sesame oil
2 tsp rice wine vinegar
1/4 tsp red pepper flakes
1/4 tsp granulated garlic
1/4 tsp sugar

Also take:
5-ounce can or 7-ounce pouch chicken

Add the vegetable and 6 cups water to a large pot, bring to a boil. Add in the pasta and cook for time on package, drain carefully. Toss with chicken (and any broth), then with the well shaken up sauce.

Serves 2

Note: Look for quick cooking spaghetti, under 6 minutes. Angel hair pasta can be used instead.

Chicken Tortellini

In a quart freezer bag:
12 ounce package dry cheese tortellini
1/2 cup freeze-dried green beans

In a snack bag:
1/4 cup shelf stable Parmesan cheese
2 tsp Mrs. Dash seasoning (or similar)
1 tsp Italian seasoning blend

Also take:
7-ounce pouch chicken
2 packets or 2 Tbsp olive oil

In your pot add the tortellini bag to 4 cups water, bring to a boil. Let simmer gently for 5 minutes. Take off the stove, cover tightly and let sit for 15 minutes (in cooler temperatures use a pot cozy). Drain off the water carefully, add the oil and then seasoning bag.

Serves 2 to 3

Ramen Dishes For One

Hearty Beef and Veggie Noodles

In a sandwich or quart freezer bag:
3-ounce ramen noodle block (toss the flavor packet)
1 1/2 tsp lower sodium beef bouillon
1/4 cup freeze dried roast beef cubes
1 Tbsp diced dried carrots
1 Tbsp diced dried onions
1 tsp dried chives
1/8 tsp red pepper flakes

Also take:
1 packet soy sauce

FBC method: Add 1 1/2 cups near boiling water and the soy sauce to the freezer bag. Stir well, seal tightly and put in a cozy for 15 minutes.

Insulated mug method: In a large insulated mug add the dry ingredients, the soy sauce and 1 1/2 cups boiling water. Stir well, cover tightly and let sit for 15 minutes.

One pot method: Bring 1 1/2 cups water and the soy sauce to a boil and add in the dry ingredients. Stir well and cook gently for 3 minutes. Take off the stove and let sit tightly covered for a couple minutes. In cooler temperatures use a pot cozy.

Serves 1

Chicken Primavera Ramen

In a sandwich or quart freezer bag add:
3-ounce ramen noodle block
¼ cup freeze-dried zucchini
2 Tbsp freeze-dried or dehydrated canned chicken
2 Tbsp tomato powder
1 Tbsp diced freeze-dried or dehydrated celery
1 Tbsp freeze-dried or dehydrated bell pepper
1 1/2 tsp lower sodium chicken bouillon
1 tsp Italian herb

Also take:
2 packets Parmesan cheese

FBC method: Add 1 1/2 cups near boiling water to the freezer bag. Stir well, seal tightly and put in a cozy for 15 minutes. Sprinkle the cheese on top.

Insulated mug method: In a large insulated mug add the dry ingredients and 1 1/2 cups boiling water. Stir well, cover tightly and let sit for 15 minutes. Sprinkle the cheese on top.

One pot method: Bring 1 1/2 cups water to a boil and add in the dry ingredients. Stir well and cook gently for 3 minutes. Take off the stove and let sit tightly covered for a couple minutes. In cooler temperatures use a pot cozy. Sprinkle the cheese on top.

Serves 1

Chicken Ramen

In a sandwich or quart freezer bag:
3-ounce ramen noodle block (toss the flavor packet)
1/4 cup freeze-dried or dehydrated canned chicken
1/4 cup freeze-dried green peas
1 Tbsp dried carrot powder
1 1/2 tsp lower sodium chicken bouillon
1 tsp Worcestershire sauce powder

FBC method: Add 1 1/2 cups near boiling water to the freezer bag. Stir well, seal tightly and put in a cozy for 15 minutes.

Insulated mug method: In a large insulated mug add the dry ingredients and 1 1/2 cups boiling water. Stir well, cover tightly and let sit for 15 minutes.

One pot method: Bring 1 1/2 cups water to a boil and add in the dry ingredients. Stir well and cook gently for 3 minutes. Take off the stove and let sit tightly covered for a couple minutes. In cooler temperatures use a pot cozy.

Serves 1

Note: Find the Worcestershire sauce powder online or carry up to a Tablespoon of liquid sauce in a spill resistant bottle. It is very shelf stable and adds great flavor.

Dry Mixes & Seasonings

Dry Cream Of Mushroom Soup Mix

Mix together:
2 cups dry milk
3/4 cup cornstarch
2 Tbsp lower sodium vegetable bouillon
2 Tbsp diced dried onion
2 Tbsp crumbled dried mushrooms
1 tsp dried basil
1 tsp dried thyme
1/2 tsp ground pepper

Store in an airtight container. Makes 5 servings of 1/3 cup each. To use as a soup, combine with 1 1/4 cups cool water and stir very well in your pot over a low flame till thick. Salt to taste and add Parmesan cheese if desired.
Can be used in recipes calling for dry cream of soup mix and added in with the dry ingredients.

Dry Cream of What You Want Mix

Mix together:
1 cup dry milk
1 cup cornstarch
4 tsp lower sodium vegetable bouillon
2 Tbsp diced dried onion
1/2 tsp ground pepper

Store in an airtight container. Makes 5 servings. In your pot stir 1/3 cup mix with 1 1/4 cups cool water. Stir over a low flame till thickened. Salt to taste and add Parmesan cheese if desired.
Can be used in recipes calling for dry cream of soup mix and added in with the dry ingredients.

Notes: Works well with whatever you like added. Tomato powder added makes Cream Of Tomato, or add mushrooms, chicken, different herbs, etc. It works well for making tuna casserole on the trail.

White Sauce

In a sandwich bag:
3 Tbsp all-purpose flour
2/3 cup dry milk
1/4 tsp salt
1/4 tsp ground black pepper

Also take:
1 Tbsp or 1 packet olive oil

Blend in slowly, using a mini whisk, 2 cups cold water and the oil over a low flame till thickened.

Notes: This sauce is great start for many meals; you can add any seasonings you like, from garlic and onions to any herbs or hot sauces. You can add anything from dried hamburger to pouched meats. Adding in 2 to 4 ounces of cheese gives you a great cheese sauce.

Beef Bouillon Sauce

In a sandwich bag:
2 Tbsp all-purpose flour
2 tsp lower sodium beef bouillon
1/2 tsp Worcestershire sauce powder
Ground black pepper and salt to taste

Also take 2 Tbsp or 2 packets olive oil

Heat the oil over a low flame in your pot. Add in the flour and cook gently till browned. Slowly add in 1-cup water, whisking until blended. Let cook till bubbly and thick. Add more water till you reach the desired thickness if desired.
Season to taste.

Makes 1 to 1 1/2 cups sauce

Note: Find Worcestershire sauce powder online or carry liquid with you. Use as a base for veggies, hamburger and more.

Brown Gravy Mix

Mix together:
1 2/3 cups cornstarch
6 tablespoons lower sodium beef bouillon powder
4 tsp instant coffee powder (preferably espresso powder)
2 tsp onion powder
1 tsp granulated garlic
1/2 tsp ground black pepper
1/2 tsp paprika

Combine all ingredients in an airtight container. With lid on tightly, shake to blend.

To make gravy, measure 3 Tablespoons mix and pack in a small bag. Add 1 1/2 cups cool water to the mix in your pot. Bring to a boil and simmer 1 minute, stirring till thick.

Makes 10 batches of gravy mix

Low Sodium Bouillon Mixes:

Both of the following recipes have a chicken flavor due to the nutritional yeast. Be sure to get nutritional yeast and not brewers yeast. Brewers yeast has an unpleasant flavor. You can find it most natural food stores and many grocery stores.

#1

2 tsp freeze-dried vegetables
1/8 tsp granulated garlic
1/4 tsp onion powder
1/2 tsp celery seed
1/2 tsp poultry seasoning
1/2 tsp sugar
2 Tbsp nutritional yeast

Mix all ingredients in a blender or spice grinder till powdered. Makes 3 servings of 1 Tablespoon each. Store in a tightly sealed bag or container. Salt can be added if desired to your taste. If a recipe calls for 1 teaspoon of commercial bouillon, use 1 Tablespoon mix instead.

#2

1 1/3 cups nutritional yeast
3 Tbsp onion powder
2 1/4 tsp granulated garlic
1 tsp celery seed
3 Tbsp Italian seasoning
2 Tbsp dried parsley

Mix all ingredients, except for parsley, in a blender or spice grinder till powdered. Add in parsley and mix. Makes 16 servings of 1 Tablespoon each. Store in a tightly sealed bag or container. Salt can be added if desired to your taste. If a recipe calls for 1 teaspoon of commercial bouillon, use 1 Tablespoon of mix instead.

Vegetable Broth Mix

1 Tbsp onion powder
1 Tbsp dried celery flakes
1 Tbsp dried parsley flakes
1 1/2 tsp granulated garlic
1/2 tsp salt
1/2 tsp ground savory
1/2 tsp dried marjoram
1/2 tsp dried thyme
1/4 tsp pepper
1/4 tsp turmeric powder
1/4 tsp ground sage

Combine all ingredients in a small bowl, cover tightly and shake to mix. Store in and airtight container. Shake well before using. Use in place of vegetable bouillon if desired or to add flavor to many recipes.

Makes 1/4 cup

Note: This recipe does not contain nutritional yeast. It contains kosher salt as well, for a total of 960 mg of sodium for the whole batch. Serving size depends on how much you prefer, from 1 teaspoon to 1 Tablespoon.

Garlic Tarragon Parmesan Cheese

1/2 cup shelf stable Parmesan cheese
1 tsp crumbled dried tarragon
1 tsp granulated garlic
1 tsp dried parsley

Stir together all the ingredients. Package mixture in an airtight container and store in the refrigerator till trip time. Package in small bags or add directly to meals being prepped. Use the same amount for when Parmesan cheese is called for.

Pesto Butter Powder

3 Tbsp butter powder
2 Tbsp shelf stable Parmesan cheese
1 tsp dried basil
1/2 tsp dried parsley
1/4 tsp granulated garlic

Combine butter powder, Parmesan cheese and herbs. Seal in a tightly sealed bag or hard container. Store in the refrigerator till trip time. Package in small bags or add directly to meals being prepped.

Italian Parmesan Herb Mix

8 ounces shelf stable Parmesan cheese
3 Tbsp crumbled dried Italian herb blend
3 Tbsp dried parsley
1 Tbsp granulated garlic
1/2 tsp ground pepper

Stir together all the ingredients. Package mixture in an airtight container and store in the refrigerator till trip time. Package in small bags or add directly to meals being prepped. Use the same amount for when Parmesan cheese is called for.

Parma "Cheese" Topper

In a blender whirl till combined:
1/4 cup nutritional yeast
1/4 cup sesame seeds
1/4 tsp sea salt, if desired

Store in a tightly sealed container, in a dry cool place. Use 1 to 2 Tablespoon as a serving.

This recipe is a nice topper for soups, rice and pasta dishes. You have to be open to trying new tastes and know that while it doesn't replace cheese it is still very tasty and will give you Vitamin B12 & other nutrients in your meals and is vegan friendly.

Munchy Crunchies

For the vegetables, use freeze-dried vegetables, not traditional dehydrated.

Combine and mix in a bowl:
1/2 cup freeze-dried onions
1/2 cup freeze-dried carrots
1/2 cup freeze-dried bell peppers
1/2 cup diced sun-dried tomatoes

Add in:
1/4 cup roasted sunflower seeds
1/4 cup roasted soy nuts
1/2 cup bacon bits (real or soy TVP 'bacon')

This makes about 3 cups of Munchy Crunchies. Store tightly sealed in small bags; 1/4 cup is a good serving size.

Bring a small snack bag of them with you on trips and sprinkle on top of your dinners, on soups or just eat as a trail snack (the new gorp?).

Options: For lower sodium leave out the bacon bits and bump up nuts. To keep nearly sodium free, use unsalted nuts and seeds. For a change of pace consider adding in diced dried fruit such as tart cherries or cranberries.

Salsa Pico De Gallo

At home mix together in a glass bowl:

14 ounce can tomatoes, drained
4 ounce can diced green Chile peppers, drained
3/4 cup chopped onion
1 Tbsp fresh lime juice
1/4 tsp dried diced garlic or 1 large clove diced
3/4 tsp dried oregano
1/4 tsp ground black pepper
3 Tbsp fresh or 3 tsp dry cilantro

Process till chunky smooth in a food chopper or blender. Spread on a parchment paper lined dehydrator tray. Dry at 135* till dry (no sticky or wet spots, it will be like fruit leather.) When dry, either break up, or whirl in a blender to powder if desired.

Recipe makes about 2 cups fresh. When ready to rehydrate start with equal amounts cool water to dried product and add water till desired texture.

A serving size is 1 to 2 Tablespoons of dried mix. Carry it in snack size zip top bags. You can use cold or hot water to rehydrate.

Great in quesadillas, on rice dishes, or wherever you want an extra something added to a dish. I like adding it to instant rice, and then putting it on wraps.

DIY Instant Salsa

In a snack size bag:
1/4 cup diced sun-dried tomatoes
1 Tbsp diced dried shallots or onions
1 Tbsp tomato powder
2 tsp diced dried jalapeños
3 packets True Lime powder
1/2 tsp sugar
1/4 tsp diced dried garlic
1/4 tsp ground pepper
Pinch of salt

Add 3/4 cup cool water, stirring well and seal tightly. Let sit for 30 minutes to an hour, to rehydrate. Knead the bag gently every 10 minutes or so.

Makes 1-cup salsa. This is a considerable amount; you may want to halve the recipe. For spicier salsa, up the jalapeños to a Tablespoon. This would work well with part of the tomatoes replaced with diced dried bell peppers or freeze-dried mango.

Cranberry Sauce

In a small bag:
1/4 cup dried sweetened cranberries
2 tsp sugar
1/2 cup water

Combine all ingredients in a small pot and bring to a boil. Reduce heat and simmer for about 8 minutes or until the cranberries start looking a little saucy

Note: it will appear somewhat soupy, but will thicken once cooled. Eat warm or allow to cool for a thicker sauce.

Low Sodium "Soy Sauce"

3/4 cup garlic vinegar
3 Tbsp dark molasses
3 tsp onion powder (not onion salt)

Mix together in a sterile small jar. Store in the refrigerator for up to a month. Makes a shy 1-cup.

Carry in a leak proof container and use when soy sauce is called for in recipes. It adds a nice spike of flavor without sodium or MSG and is great sprinkled on rice and pasta dishes or to dip California rolls into.

Notes: This is a great ultra low sodium alternative to the real item. While one can get lower sodium soy sauce commercially it is still very high in sodium.

Tomato leather
-For homemade tomato powder

1 small onion, minced
2 garlic cloves, minced
1 Tbsp olive oil
12 ounces tomato paste (unsalted if desired)
1 tsp sugar
2 tsp parsley, chopped or 1 Tbsp dry
Ground black pepper, to taste
1/4 tsp dried basil

Sauté onions and garlic in oil until soft and golden. Add remaining ingredients and cook slowly for 10 minutes over medium heat. If bubbling too much, turn to low.

Spread tomato mixture on a parchment paper lined dehydrator tray. Dry at 135-140* for about 6 hours. When dry (pliable but not sticky) let cool. Freeze for an hour and then whirl in a blender to powder and store in a tightly sealed plastic bag. It may be frozen for longer storage.

To rehydrate for tomato sauce, add a ratio of 1:3 of dried product to water. For example, if you need 3 Tablespoons of tomato sauce use 1 Tablespoon dried tomato powder and 3 Tablespoons water. For tomato paste use a ratio of 1:2.

It can be used as a powder in any recipe that calls for "tomato powder". It adds depth and flavor to many recipes as well. If desired, one can salt to taste.

Alfredo Sauce Mix

1 cup dry milk
2 Tbsp shelf stable Parmesan cheese
1/3 cup diced dried onion
1 tsp granulated garlic
1/4 tsp salt, if desired
1/2 tsp white pepper

Mix all the ingredients together and store in a tightly sealed bag or container.

Use in place of commercial "Dry Alfredo Mix" when called for in recipes. Depending on your taste you may want to add more salt.

This mix adds a nice perk of flavor sprinkling 1 to 2 Tablespoon of it into rice, mashed potatoes, couscous and soup mixes.

Onion Soup Mix

3 Tbsp diced dried onion
1 tsp onion powder
4 tsp low sodium bouillon (Beef or vegetable)
1/4 tsp celery seed
1/4 tsp ground black pepper
Salt to taste

Mix all ingredients together and store in a tightly sealed bag or container. The mix is equivalent to a commercial envelope that will make 4 cups of liquid soup.
Add to rice and other starch dishes to give flavor without added MSG or heavy sodium. Depending on your taste you may want to add 1/4 to 1/2 teaspoon salt to the mix.

Parmesan Cheese Sauce Mix

1 cup dry milk
4 Tbsp shelf stable Parmesan or Romano cheese
1/2 tsp onion powder
1 1/2 tsp granulated garlic
1/2 tsp pepper

Mix all ingredients together and store in a tightly sealed bag or container. Makes about 5 servings of 1/4 cup each. Keeps for up to 4 months, stored away from heat. For long term storage keep in the refrigerator.

To use: Combine 1/4 cup mix with 2 Tablespoons melted butter or olive oil and 1/4 cup water. Add salt in camp to taste.

This mix works well with cooked and dehydrated pasta. 1/4 cup of the dry mix makes enough sauce for 4 ounces of dehydrated pasta. (Weight after cooking and drying the pasta)

Other types of dried cheeses can be found online to substitute for the Parmesan. Use dehydrated cheese, not freeze-dried.

Instant Pesto Mix

In a small bag mix together:
3 Tbsp dried basil
2 Tbsp shelf stable Parmesan cheese
1 to 3 tsp dried diced garlic

Also take 1 to 2 Tbsp or 1 to 2 packets extra virgin olive oil

Add oil to the bag; mix with spoon to a paste. Drizzle in warm water - about 2 to 3 Tablespoons, depending on how much oil you used. Stir and let sit for 5 minutes to rehydrate and blend flavors.

You can use cold water as well, allowing 10 minutes to rehydrate.

1 serving, of about a quarter cup, when mixed up. The garlic amount is up to the user, depending on how string you like it. A couple grinds of black pepper is nice as well.

Instant Spaghetti Sauce

In a pint freezer bag:
1/4 cup tomato powder
2 Tbsp shelf stable Parmesan cheese
1 Tbsp diced sun-dried tomatoes
1 tsp diced dried onion
1/2 tsp Italian seasoning
1/2 tsp sugar
1/4 tsp granulated garlic
1/8 to 1/4 tsp salt

Also take 1 Tbsp or 1 packet extra virgin olive oil

Add the oil and 1 cup very warm water to the bag. Stir well, seal tightly and let sit in a cozy for 15 minutes.
Use as a sauce base for dishes or toss with 4 to 6 ounces hot pasta. To make vegan, leave out the cheese.

Serves 1

Taco Seasoning Mix

2 tsp dried onion
1 tsp chili powder
1/2 tsp dried red pepper flakes
1/4 tsp dried oregano
1/4 tsp salt
1/2 tsp cornstarch
1/2 tsp dried garlic
1/2 tsp ground cumin

Mix all ingredients together and store in a tightly sealed bag or container.

Makes about 2 Tablespoon of mix.

Use in place of commercial "Taco Mix" when called for in recipes. This mix has controlled sodium and is MSG free as well. Depending on your taste you may want to add more salt.

Fajita Seasoning Mix

In a small bag mix together:
1 Tbsp cornstarch
2 tsp chili powder
1 tsp paprika
1 tsp sugar
1 tsp low sodium Beef bouillon
1/2 tsp onion powder
1/4 tsp garlic powder
1/4 tsp cayenne pepper
1/4 tsp ground cumin
1/4 tsp salt, if desired.

Seal tightly. Use in recipes calling for commercial fajita mix or sprinkle on meals that need a kick. The cornstarch thickens nicely into a sauce.

Desserts, Energy Bars & Balls

Fruit Fritters

In a quart freezer bag:
1 cup all-purpose flour
1 Tbsp baking powder
2 Tbsp granulated sugar
2 Tbsp commercial dried eggs
1/3 cup dry milk

In a sandwich bag:
1 cup dried mixed fruit, diced

Also take:
2 Tbsp or 2 packets vegetable oil
1 new brown paper linch bag
1/2 cup granulated sugar

Cover the dried fruit with 1 cup cool water, seal tightly and let sit for at least 30 minutes to soften up. Drain and reserve the water left into a cup, measuring 1/2 cup. Add the reserved water to the dry ingredients, kneading through the bag to combine, add in the fruit till mixed in thoroughly.

Heat the oil, a Tablespoon at a time, over a low flame in a non-stick fry pan lid. Add in the dough by spoonfuls and cook till browned, flipping to cook both sides. Cook 2 batches, adding in the other Tablespoon of oil for the second batch.

Add the sugar to the bag, toss in the hot treats, fold over and shake to coat.

Serves 2 to 4

Cobbler Pudding

In a sandwich bag:
3/4 cup small chopped dried fruit or berries (what you like)
2 Tbsp dry milk
1 Tbsp instant tapioca
1 Tbsp packed brown sugar
1/2 tsp ground cinnamon
1/4 tsp ground nutmeg

In a snack size bag:
1/2 cup vanilla wafer cookies, finely crumbled
2 Tbsp candied pecans, finely chopped

Add 1 cup water and first bag to your pot and bring to a boil. Take off the stove, cover tightly and let sit for 15 minutes. Top with the cookie mix and let sit for another 5 minutes. Stir in the topping to combine.

Serves 1 to 2

Berry and Fruit Rice Pudding

In a sandwich bag:
1 cup instant rice
1/4 cup diced dried fruit and berries mix

In a snack size bag:
1/2 box instant vanilla pudding mix (preferably all natural)
2 Tbsp dry milk
1/4 tsp ground cinnamon

Bring 1 3/4 cups water and the rice bag to a boil. Cover tightly and let sit for 10 minutes, it will appear watery. Stir in the pudding bag till smooth and thickened.

Serves 2

Apple Dumplings

In a snack bag:
2/3 cup baking mix
1 Tbsp sugar
1/2 tsp cinnamon

In a sandwich bag:
2 cups sugar
1/4 cup cornstarch
1 tsp cinnamon
1/2 tsp True Lemon or 1 packet lemon juice
6 ounces (2 cups) dried soft apple slices or rings
Pinch of salt

Add 1/4 cup of the water to the baking mix bag. Knead gently till mixed.

In a 2 Liter pot add the apples the sugar bag and 3 cups water and bring to a boil.
Squeeze the dumplings on top, cover and cook simmering for 10 minutes. Take off the heat and let sit for 5 more minutes.

Serves 2 to 4, depending on appetite

Blueberry Cheesecake

In a quart freezer bag:
1 4 serving package instant cheesecake pudding mix
2/3 cup instant milk

In a sandwich bag:
3/4 cup dried blueberries
1/4 cup sugar
1/2 tsp dried lemon zest

In a snack size zip top bag:
1 cup granola (a sweet variety is best)

Add 1/4 cup water, blueberries, sugar and lemon rind to your pot and bring to a boil. Take off the stove and set aside to cool.
Add 1 3/4 cups cold water to the pudding bag. Seal tightly and shake till well blended (a couple minutes). Stash the pudding in a cold creek or snowfield to chill for at least 10 minutes.
Split the pudding between mugs (or you can use 4 clean snack size bags for easy clean up), divide the blueberry topping over it. Sprinkle granola on top.

Serves 4

Trail Dessert Quesadillas

Take with you:
2 flour tortillas
1/2 cup marshmallows
2 Tbsp chocolate chips
1/2 tsp cinnamon sugar

Put your pot lid over low heat on your stove.
Meanwhile sprinkle the marshmallows and chocolate chips evenly over the two tortillas. Sprinkle with the sugar. Top with the second tortilla. Cook the tortillas for 1 to 3 minutes or until lightly browned, then carefully flip it and cook on the other side for an additional 1 to 3 minutes or until nicely brown and melty. Be sure to watch the heat and keep the pan above the stove if needed to prevent burning. Remove the tortillas off the stove.

No lid to use? You can always wrap them in aluminum foil and leave on a rock by a fire to melt. Or you can eat 'em cold!

Serves 1 to 2

Peanut Butter S'more Quesadillas

Take:
1/4 cup peanut butter
2 flour tortillas
1/2 cup miniature marshmallows
1/4 cup chocolate chips
1 medium bananas, thinly sliced, if desired

In camp spread half of the peanut butter over half of each tortilla.
Sprinkle marshmallows and chocolate over peanut butter.
Top with banana slices, if desired.
Fold tortillas in half, press gently to flatten and seal.

Put your pot lid over low heat on your stove if your pan has one. Put one quesadilla in; cook for 1 to 3 minutes on each side or until golden and chocolate is melting. You may have to keep the lid above the flame so you don't burn the tortilla. Repeat with other quesadilla.

No lid to use? You can always wrap them in aluminum foil and leave on a rock by a fire to melt. Or you can eat 'em cold!

Serves 2

Blueberry Rice Pudding

In a quart freezer or sandwich bag:
2/3 cup instant rice
1/3 cup dried blueberries
3 Tbsp dry milk
3 Tbsp maple sugar
1 Tbsp butter powder
2 tsp potato starch
1/2 tsp ground cinnamon

FBC method: Add 1 cup near boiling water and stir well. Seal tightly and put in a cozy for 15 to 20 minutes. Stir well before serving.

Insulated mug method: Add 1-cup boiling water and stir well. Cover tightly and let sit for 15 to 20 minutes. Stir well before serving.

One pot method: Bring 1 cup water to a boil in your pot. Turn off the stove and add in the dry ingredients, stirring well. Cover tightly and let sit for 15 minutes. In cold temperatures, insulate the pot in a pot cozy.

Serves 1 to 2

Tapioca Pudding

In a sandwich bag:
2/3 cup dry milk
3 Tbsp instant tapioca
3 Tbsp sugar
1 tsp vanilla powder
1/8 tsp salt

Add the dry ingredients to your pot with 2 cups water and let sit for 15 minutes. Bring to a boil, stirring often and then cook for a minute. Take off the stove and stash in a snow bank or cold stream. The pudding will thicken as it cools.

Serves 2

Note: Find vanilla powder in stores specializing in coffee/espresso bar products. It can also be found online through baking specialty stores. If you cannot find it, use vanilla sugar or vanilla extract.

Rice Pudding

In a quart freezer bag:
2/3 cup instant rice
1/3 cup raisins
1/4 cup brown sugar
3 Tbsp dry milk
1 tsp potato starch
1/4 tsp cinnamon

FBC method: Add 1 cup near boiling water. Stir well, seal tightly and put in a cozy for 15 minutes.

Mug method: Add 1 cup boiling water to the dry ingredients. Stir well, cover tightly and let sit for 15 minutes.

One pot method: Bring 1 cup water to a boil in your pot. Add in the dry ingredients, stirring well. Turn off the stove and cover tightly and let sit for 10 minutes. In cold weather insulate in a pot cozy.

Serves 2 as a desert, 1 for breakfast

Homemade Pudding

In a sandwich bag:
1/2 cup dry milk
1/4 cup sugar
3 Tbsp cornstarch
1/2 tsp vanilla powder
1/8 tsp salt

Also take 1 Tbsp butter or margarine

Add the mix and 2 cups cold water to your pot. Using a small whisk stir well while bringing to a boil. As soon as it boils and is thick, pull off the stove and whisk in the butter.
Serve warm or chill in a snow bank or cold stream.

Serves 2 to 4 depending on appetite

Notes: Find vanilla powder where coffee/espresso products are sold or online through gourmet baking supply sites. For an easy banana pudding add in 2 Tbsp powdered freeze-dried bananas with the dry ingredients and top with vanilla wafer cookies.

Pan Brownies

In a quart freezer bag:
1/4 cup all-purpose flour
3 Tbsp granulated sugar
2 Tbsp mini chocolate baking chips
1 Tbsp unsweetened cocoa powder
1 Tbsp finely diced candied nuts, pecans or walnuts
1 1/2 tsp dry milk
1/4 tsp baking powder
pinch of kosher salt

Also take 1 Tbsp or 1 packet vegetable oil

Add 3 Tablespoons cold water to the bag and a drizzle of the oil. Seal and knead gently till combined. Heat a wide 2L pot or fry pan lid over a low flame, add in the rest of the oil, heating through. Use your knife and rip off the corner of the bag, squeezing the dough into the pan. Cook until the bottom is browned, using your spoon or spatula to cut into quarters. Flip over and cook till browned as well. Keep a close eye on them to prevent scorching.

Serves 1 to 2

Bananas Foster

In a quart freezer bag put:
1 cup freeze-dried bananas (sliced)
2 Tbsp brown sugar
1 Tbsp butter powder
1 Tbsp potato starch
1/2 tsp vanilla powder
1/2 tsp cinnamon
1/2 tsp True Lemon powder

FBC method: Bring 1 cup water to a near boil. Add to the ingredients stirring well. Seal tightly and put in a cozy for 15 minutes. Stir again.

Insulated mug method: Add 1 cup boiling water to the dry ingredients. Stir well, cover tightly and let sit for 15 minutes. Stir again.

Serves 1 to 2

Note: This pudding like dessert is also tasty used as a topping over trail pancakes!

Applesauce

In a sandwich bag:
1 cup dried chopped apples
1 cup brown sugar
1/4 cup raisins
1/2 tsp ground cinnamon
1/4 tsp ground nutmeg

Add the ingredients to your pot, cover with water and bring to a boil.
Take off the stove and let sit tightly covered for 5 minutes.

Serves 2

Note: The applesauce can be used as a topper over pancakes as well.
Start with 1-cup water, add more as needed.

Simmered Cherries

In a sandwich bag:
6 ounce package dried tart cherries
6 Tbsp sugar
3 Tbsp instant tapioca
1/2 tsp True Lemon or Lime powder (2 packets)
1/2 tsp ground cinnamon

Add the dry ingredients to your pot with 2 cups water and let sit for 15 minutes to soak. Bring to a boil and cook for a minute. Take off the stove and cool in a snow bank or a cold stream. It will thicken as it cools.

Serves 2

Note: This is a great sauce served over pound cake or pancakes

Huckleberry Dessert

In a sandwich bag pack:
1/2 cup sugar
2 Tbsp all-purpose flour
1 tsp ground cinnamon
1 tsp dried lemon zest
1/4 tsp True Lemon powder
1 Tbsp butter powder

Pick 2 cups fresh Huckleberries or wild Blueberries in camp.

Mix half the berries and the dry ingredients in a pot with 2 Tablespoons water and bring to a slow boil over a low flame, simmer for 10 minutes on the lowest flame you can dial down to. Stir in the rest of the berries and let cool for 30 minutes. If you happened to pack in some pound cake or even Twinkies, even better - top it with the sauce. Or serve over hot pancakes.

Serves 2 to 3

Cookies In A Pot

In a sandwich bag:
1 Tbsp dry milk
1 cups sugar
1 1/2 Tbsp cocoa powder

Also take:
3 Tbsp peanut butter (2 packets)
1/4 cup butter or margarine

In a sandwich bag:
1 1/2 cups quick cooking oats

In your pot add ¼ cup water, the butter and milk bag and bring to a boil.
Remove from the heat and stir in peanut butter till melted, then quickly add the oats. Stir well and press compactly into the bottom of the pot, let cool.

Makes enough for 2 to 3, depending on appetite

Hot Chocolate Pudding in a Mug

Pack in a snack bag:
1/4 cup dry milk
2 Tbsp semi sweet mini chocolate chips
1 Tbsp sugar
1 Tbsp cocoa powder
1 Tbsp potato starch
1/2 tsp vanilla powder
Pinch salt

Add 1-cup boiling water; stir well and let sit till cool enough to drink. The drink will start thickening instantly and be a cross between a thick drink and warm pudding.

Serves 1

Hot Chai Pudding in a Mug

Pack in a snack bag:
1/2 cup dry milk
1 Tbsp butter powder
1 Tbsp potato starch
2 tsp sugar
1/2 tsp ground ginger
1/2 tsp ground cinnamon
1/4 tsp ground cardamom
Pinch of kosher salt

Add 1-cup boiling water; stir well and let sit till cool enough to drink. The drink will start thickening instantly and be a cross between a thick drink and warm pudding.

Serves 1

Peanut Butter Granola Balls

Ingredients:
1/3 cup honey or agave nectar
1/4 cup natural peanut butter
2 Tbsp butter
1 cup crisp rice cereal
1 cup old-fashioned rolled oats
1/4 cup diced dried fruit

At home:
In a pot over medium heat warm up the honey, peanut butter, and butter. Stir until melted and smooth, a couple minutes. Remove from the heat; stir in cereal, oats, and dried fruit. Drop mixture by spoonfuls onto a parchment paper lined baking sheet. Let set up for an hour and then store tightly covered in the refrigerator till trail time. Carry in a small plastic box to protect.

How many it makes depends on size.

Nut & Chocolate Balls

Ingredients:
1/2 cup nut butter of choice
3 Tbsp cocoa powder
3 Tbsp sugar
2 Tbsp mini chocolate chips
1 tsp pure vanilla extract

Extra cocoa powder

At home:
Mix everything in a medium bowl. Scoop out balls (any size) of the mix and drop in a bowl of the extra cocoa powder. Roll gently to cover. Store tightly covered in the refrigerator till trail time. Carry in a small plastic box to protect.

How many it makes depends on size.

Cinnamon Granola Bars

Ingredients:
1/4 cup butter, softened
1 cup packed dark brown sugar
1 large egg
2 Tbsp ground flaxseed
2 Tbsp agave nectar or honey
2 cups old-fashioned rolled oats
1 cup all-purpose flour
1 tsp ground cinnamon
1/2 tsp baking soda
1/2 raisins

Heat oven to 350 and spray a 9x13" baking dish with cooking spray or lightly oil.

In a large bowl beat the butter and brown sugar till well mixed. Beat the egg in, then the flax and agave. In a small bowl whisk the oats, flour, cinnamon and baking soda together, stir into the butter mixture until blended. Stir in the raisins. Press into the prepared baking dish and bake for 15 to 20 minutes or until the edges are lightly browned.

Cut into 12 bars. When cool wrap in plastic wrap for carrying.

Coconut Pecan Cereal Bars

Ingredients:
7 ounces shredded coconut
1 1/2 cups pecan halves
10 ounces marshmallows
4 Tbsp butter
4 cups cornflakes

At home:
Preheat oven to 350. Spread coconut on one side of a baking sheet, and pecans on other side. Toast until fragrant about 15 to 20 minutes, tossing occasionally (but keeping separated). Meanwhile, coat an 8-inch square-baking pan with cooking spray or oil; line with a strip of parchment paper (leaving an overhang on two sides). Spray paper with more cooking spray.

In a large nonstick pot over medium-low, heat marshmallows and butter until melted, 5 to 10 minutes, stirring frequently. Stir in the cornflakes, coconut, and pecans. Quickly pack into the prepared pan with a spatula and let cool until firm. Remove from pan; peel off paper. Using a serrated knife, cut into squares. Wrap tightly in plastic and eat within a couple days.

Makes 9 large squares.

Cranberry Oat Cereal Bars

Ingredients:
4 Tbsp butter
10 ounces marshmallows
1/4 tsp salt
6 cups toasted oat cereal
1 cup dried cranberries

At home:
Spray a 9" x 13" glass pan with cooking spray or oil. Line with parchment paper; spray paper with cooking spray and set aside.

In a large saucepan, melt butter over medium heat. Add marshmallows and salt; cook, stirring occasionally, until marshmallows have melted, about 5 minutes. Remove from heat and stir in cereal and cranberries. Quickly pack into the prepared pan with a spatula and let cool until firm. Remove from pan; peel off paper. Using a serrated knife, cut into squares. Wrap tightly in plastic and eat within a couple days.

Makes as many as you cut, 16 to 24 on average.

Trail Mix Cookies

Ingredients:
1 cup old-fashioned rolled oats
1 1/4 cups all-purpose flour
1 tsp baking soda
1 tsp salt
1 cup unsweetened applesauce
1/2 cup unsalted butter (1 stick)
3/4 cup white sugar
3/4 cup brown sugar, packed
1 tsp pure vanilla extract
2 large eggs
12 ounces semi-sweet chocolate chips (1 bag)
1 cup diced almonds
1 1/2 cups dried sweetened cranberries

Directions:
Preheat oven to 375. Beat the eggs in a large bowl and then add in dry ingredients in order. Scoop large Tablespoon size cookies on an ungreased cookie sheet. Bake for 10 to 12 minutes or until golden brown. Let cool on racks, then wrap tightly.

No Bake Chocolate Peanut Butter Oatmeal Bars

Ingredients:
9 ounces chocolate wafers (about 40), finely ground to make 2 cups
1 1/2 cups old-fashioned rolled oats
1 1/4 cups powdered sugar
10 Tbsp (1 ¼ sticks) unsalted butter
1 cup chunky peanut butter
1 cup smooth peanut butter
12 ounces semisweet chocolate chips

Spray cooking spray or butter a 9x13" pan, setting aside. Mix the wafers, oats and sugar in a medium bowl. Meanwhile, melt the butter in a small saucepan over medium heat, then add the chunky peanut butter and 3/4 cup of the smooth peanut butter, whisk till smooth. Add the peanut butter mixture to the wafer blend, stirring until mixed. Pack into the pan and press down firmly. Refrigerate for 30 minutes.

Melt 10 ounces of the chocolate, spread over the bars in a thin layer. Refrigerate for 15 minutes to harden.

Melt the remaining smooth peanut butter and chocolate in separate containers and drizzle over the top. Refrigerate for 15 minutes to harden.

Slice into bars, storing refrigerator for up to a week or a month in the freezer. These are better for cool weather trips as they will soften in warm weather.

3 Ingredient Nut Butter Balls

Ingredients:
2 Tbsp old-fashioned oats
2 Tbsp natural peanut butter or favorite nut butter
2 tsp agave syrup or honey

Directions:
Whirl the oats in a blender or food chopper till finely ground. Add the peanut butter and agave. Mix well with a spoon and form into small balls. Store in an airtight container or a plastic bag.

Ingredients:

Wondering what something is? Can you use something similar? Where can you expect to find this product? Are there DIY versions I can make?

• Canned chicken comes in cans in 3 ounces, 5 ounce and also 10 to 13 ounces. The 5-ounce size is good for 2 person meals. The broth in the can has good flavor for the meals, do not drain it. Be sure to get the cans with pull tops. While you might think that cans are heavy, once empty they weigh about the same as the foil packets. Stomp the can hard with your boot, and it will fit nicely in your garbage bag. Pouch chicken comes in 7-ounce foil packets.

• Ham comes in 7 oz foil pouches in some areas. You can also find it in small cans, look for pop-tops. Canned ham dries easily and freeze-dried can be found online.

• Tuna comes in foil pouches and cans. Pouches are preferable, as they don't need draining. 3-ounce size is perfect for one person, the 6-ounce size for two. Albacore is the better choice. If you are doing long days, use the oil packed version in pop-top cans. Tuna steaks are now available in pouches, as are flavored tuna.

• Salmon: 3-ounce pouches for 1 person, larger 7-ounce pouches are for 2 persons. Canned can be used, make sure it is boned and skin free, preferably with a pop-top.

• Seafood: Shrimp, Clams, Crab, all come in cans, but need a can opener often, use the clam juice in meals, drain shrimp and crab before using.

• You can substitute canned products for pouched items, look for pop tops. The liquid can often be used in your meal, so no draining needed.

• Hamburger: Precooked and dehydrated at home, use high quality lean meat. Freeze-dried hamburger and 'beef' flavored TVP can be found online to use instead.

- Freeze-dried meat: There are many choices, and it can be an easy way to carry meat on long trips. Freeze-dried meats are not inexpensive though, but if you are trying to save weight and space, they can be worth it. Substitute flavored TVP, which comes in 'beef', 'chicken' and 'ham' flavors. Include a 1:1 ratio of ingredient to water when cooking.

- Couscous: It is tiny pasta, full of protein and carbs, and needs only water added. Many stores carry whole wheat also. You can find this at grocery stores near the rice mixes, in bulk sections, natural food stores. Gluten-free rice "couscous is not instant and must be cooked.

- Coconut Cream Powder: A high fat and calorie powder that makes coconut cream. It is found in Asian stores and some larger ethnic sections in grocery stores, also online. Used in curry dishes to make creamier. Most do contain dairy, so read packaging carefully if you avoid it.

- Instant Hummus is a powder you mix with cold water, to make a spread. Made from chickpeas and spices. Can be found in natural or ethnic section at grocery stores, in bulk, natural food stores. Our series of Freezer Bag Cooking cookbooks contain recipes for making your own and drying.

- Instant refried beans or flakes: They come in brown or black bean. Can be found in bulk, in grocery stores, in natural food stores. Sometimes sold as "bean soup" mixes in pouches and tubs, these can be used to make refried beans. Use more water than the box calls for, as refried style, they can be very thick. Nonfat refried beans in cans may be dehydrated and used as well.

- Veggie Flakes/Dried Veggies/freeze-dried veggies: Tiny shreds of dried veggies. Usually is a mix including carrots, celery, onions, parsley, sometimes also tomato, potato, peas, beans, etc. Found in the bulk sections of grocery stores or natural food stores, sometimes sold as "soup starters". You can also find this online through some retailers. You can make your own by dehydrating a 16 oz bag of frozen mixed veggies (small cut), then chopping up in a food processor or blender.

- Dried Mushrooms: There are many kinds to try. Plain white mushrooms work well in many meals. Find in the produce department in grocery stores and online.

- Dried Bell Pepper: Dried, in small flakes, these rehydrate quite fast. Either in green or red. Some natural food stores carry, or at spice and herb stores, as well as online stores.

- Dried Onions: You want the smaller pieces (some places carry two sizes). Find at grocery stores, in bulk sections, at club stores and online.

- Dried Tomatoes/Powder: You can find dried tomatoes (sun dried, no oil) in bulk herb sections & gourmet sections. If you cannot find powder, you can run tomato pieces thru a mill, coffee grinder or food processor. You can also dry tomato paste and powder it.

- Dried Carrots: Online, spice & herb stores, in natural food stores sometimes. If you dry your own, just run through the blender or food processor till flaked.

- Instant Milk Powder: Non-fat milk is widely found, whole milk (Nido®) can be found online, at Walmart Supercenters® or in gourmet cooking stores in the baking area. For higher protein, you can use soy milk powder, found in tubs in the soymilk section of your grocery store.

- Soy Milk Powder: Instant dairy milk can be used instead. Find the soy in your grocery store in tubs, in the soy aisle. Usually is 2 Tbsp per 8 oz of liquid, so in many recipes if it calls for 1/2 cup dairy milk powder, use 2 Tbsp instead. Much higher in protein than dairy. Better Than Milk® is an excellent brand.

- Freeze-dried fruit: Look in club stores, grocery stores and online.

- Making Your Own Oatmeal: Take 1 minute "Quick" oats and run through a blender or food processor till it looks like instant oatmeal. Use the same as the instant packets, adding spices, sugar, fruit, nuts, etc.

•   Low Sodium Chicken/Vegetable/Beef Bouillon: If you use it and like salt, add a pinch of salt to your food. By using low sodium, you can control the salt to your liking. See the Dry Mixes and Seasoning section for recipes.

•   Salt: We use kosher and sea salt in our recipes. Table salt can be used, but tends to have a "saltier" flavor, use a lighter hand.

•   Instant Rice: Basic Minute Rice®. In any rice recipe you can use instant brown rice. Brown rice does need to sit in the cozy for an extra 5 to 10 minutes to fully rehydrate.

•   Cheese Sauce Powder: You can find this in bulk at some grocery stores, or online. You can always sub cheese powder packets from mac and cheese boxes or use a cheese of your choice (1 to 2 ounces) diced up. Look in organic sections for faux cheese sauce powder as well. See the Dry Mixes and Seasoning section for recipes. Some brands contain artificial coloring, read labels.

•   Salsa can be dried at home on a dehydrator but can also be found online in ready to use dry mixes. See the Dry Mixes and Seasoning section for recipes.

Resources:

The companies below we have used numerous times for both home and trail cooking and for our book's and website recipe developments. Many products mentioned in this book can be found in mainstream grocery, natural food stores and Asian grocery stores. Outdoor stores such as REI and natural food stores often carry items such as individual nut butter packets and freeze-dried fruits and vegetables. Everything can be found online, with reasonable shipping prices often with lowered or free shipping if you order over a set price amount. The ability to order easily what you seek has made planning for trips easy, frustration free and most of all allowed everyone access to fun gourmet foods.

Harmony House Foods for dehydrated beans, flavored TVP, fruits and vegetables.
http://www.harmonyhousefoods.com

Just Tomatoes produces both regular and organic freeze-dried and dehydrated vegetables and fruits.
http://www.justtomatoes.com

Crunchies Food produces a line of freeze-dried vegetables.
http://crunchiesfood.com

Looking for single serving condiments? Minimus carries nearly everything you could want from condiments, dressing, pouched meats and even supplies for your first aid kit.
http://www.minimus.biz

For those gourmet ingredients like soy sauce powder, freeze-dried meat, a vast array of vegetables and fruits and much more visit the hiker's online grocery store:
http://www.packitgourmet.com

Organic alternatives for packaged seasonings and mixes? Simply Organic Foods is a great source:
http://www.simplyorganicfoods.com

Spices, herbs, dried vegetables, dried cheese & more, often in organic versions:
http://www.frontiercoop.com

Instant beans, couscous, hummus mix & more. All natural and easy to use:
http://www.fantasticfoods.com

Instant and all natural hummus, couscous, soups and more:
http://www.casbahnaturalfoods.com

All organic instant bean flakes, instant salsa, hummus and more from Mary Jane's Organics.
http://www.maryjanesfarm.org

Nut butters in single serving packets; Justin's is our favorite:
http://www.justinsnutbutter.com

Wilderness Dining offers a selection of many brands lines, including instant salsa:
http://www.wildernessdining.com

An in depth selection of spices and herbs from around the world:
http://worldspice.com

Road's End Organics produces vegan organic gravy mixes and vegan 'cheese' toppings:
http://www.chreese.com

Asian ingredients and supplies from Thailand, Japan and more:
http://importfood.com

Many hard to find food items can be found online through Amazon:
http://www.amazon.com

Food dehydrators:
Nesco: http://www.nesco.com
Excalibur: http://www.excaliburdehydrator.com
L'EQUIP: http://www.kitchenresource.com
Amazon is an excellent place to shop for one:
http://www.amazon.com

For drying tips and how-to check out our in-depth help online at:
http://www.trailcooking.com/dehydrating-101/ and
http://blog.trailcooking.com/category/trail-cooking/dehydrating/

Index:

Introduction

Fry Pan Recipes:

Dinners

Rice Dishes:

Ramen Dishes For One:

About The Author

Sarah lives in a small, but growing, town in the foothills of Mt. Rainier, in Washington State, with her husband Kirk, and three sons, Ford, Walker and Alistaire.

Her favorite hiking areas are the Washington Cascade Mountains and Mount Rainier National Park.

She can be found online at www.gazingin.com, www.trailcooking.com and http://blog.trailcooking.com/ and on Facebook at www.facebook.com/pages/Freezer-Bag-Cooking/ and Twitter at https://twitter.com/trailcooking.

If you have any questions or comments, please email her at sarah@trailcooking.com.

Photo courtesy Janelle Walker.

Made in the
USA
Columbia, SC